"Lauren  defining her own world and learning to tune out the faulty expectations meant to hold her back. Her voice is a much-needed comfort to anyone trying to do the same. *Unboxed* is an absolute pleasure!"

-EMILY LYNN PAULSON, BESTSELLING AUTHOR OF *HIGHLIGHT REAL: FINDING HONESTY & RECOVERY BEYOND THE FILTERED LIFE,* TEDX SPEAKER AND THE FOUNDER OF SOBER MOM SQUAD®

UNBOXED

Lauren Schwarzfeld

Copyright © 2022 by Lauren Schwarzfeld

All rights reserved.

No part of this book may be reproduced in any form or by any electronic or mechanical means, including information storage and retrieval systems, without written permission from the author, except for the use of brief quotations in a book review.

ISBN: 978-1-956955-11-8 (e-book)

ISBN: 978-1-956955-12-5 (paperback)

DISCLAIMER

This work is non-fiction and, as such, reflects the author's memory of the experiences. Many of the names and identifying characteristics of the individuals featured in this book have been changed to protect their privacy, and certain individuals are composites. Dialogue and events have been recreated; in some cases, conversations were edited to convey their substance rather than written exactly as they occurred.

EXTRA RESOURCES FOR YOUR JOURNEY

This book is about a journey, a process, and I hope you'll stay with me beyond the last page.

There's no singular final destination, so we get to continue exploring all of the future "What's next?" questions together.

Scan the QR code for more resources, tools and a space for us to ask these questions together.

Let's keep going—I'd love to know what you think!

CONTENTS

Author's Note	13
Introduction	17
1. Sobriety is a Boundary *On Quitting*	23
2. Searching for the One *On Work*	33
3. Through Thick and Thin *On Marriage*	49
4. Me Plus Three *On Motherhood*	66
5. A Few Words On a Bad Word *On "Should"*	81
6. My Best Worst Friend *Or, the Story of When I Met a Narcissist*	91
7. The Take Back *On Searching*	111
8. I Joined a Cult...and It Changed My Life *On Work, Again*	123
9. Instagram versus Reality *On Social Media*	139
10. There's No Boat *On What's Next*	146
Acknowledgments	157
About the Author	161

This book is dedicated to my husband, Karl.
Sigmund Freud said, "How bold one gets when one is sure of being loved."
Thank you for fueling my boldness!
Life is so much better with you by my side.

AUTHOR'S NOTE

Hello, sweet reader.

I like context. Stories and opinions don't exist in a vacuum; they exist as part of a larger, often nuanced story. So much is lost when you try to separate the person from the stories.

So, this is who I am and where I come from.

I am a white, heterosexual, cisgender woman living in Westchester County, New York. It's among the wealthiest counties in the United States, and while I didn't grow up as part of the population that made that a reality, I've definitely benefited from it. There's an enormous difference (and great privilege) between growing up as the poor kid in an affluent area and living in a low-income community. It's different being a white kid in an affluent area. Not having assumptions made about who you are, where you come from and what your family might look like allows you a wide range of possibilities and dreams. That is my lens.

I grew up in Westchester, moved to Boston for five years for college, had a short stint in New York City and then returned to Westchester.

I've done and I continue to do work *not* to center situations around myself as I walk through this world. I write extensively about not assuming that your reality is everyone else's reality. And yet, I'm human, and I fully recognize that despite being aware of and looking out for gaps in my awareness and understanding, I do still have them. This book is my experience. It's not the only way, it's maybe not even the right way, but it's how I've come to navigate this life as I work towards feeling content, aligned and at peace—while also not being a jerk.

I approach my writing, work and life in the hopes of being honest and transparent. I'd like to think that my words and experiences might inspire you to create the life you need and want and dream of...whatever that looks like. I'm not trying to inspire you to desire or dream of my life (or anyone else's for that matter). I didn't write this book to say that if only everyone made the choices I did, we'd all be happy and successful. That is both categorically false and steeped in privilege. My goal is to help you trust yourself, believe in yourself and create a vision that both represents who you are and honors where you've been.

My life isn't marked by overwhelming hardship. I moved in with my now husband when I was 23 years old, and I haven't had real or significant money worries since. It was a stark contrast to the first part of my life, so I do not for a moment take anything I have for granted. I don't worry about putting food on the table or paying bills or getting a babysitter. Surprise expenses don't throw my world into havoc.

My journey has been comfortably uncomfortable in so many ways. The luxury of the freedom and support to be on this journey is not lost on me. When I write of situations and scenarios that I was able to navigate, I recognize both my individual power and strength to make the choices I did and also the privilege that made my options possible. The path I took and the way I took it aren't realities for so many people, and no part of this book is intended to make people feel like "we all had the same choices to make."

We don't and we didn't.

There are few things I find as infuriating as the meme that reads "You have the same 24 hours in a day as Beyoncé." No. Just a flat out *no* on that one. For each of us, our starting points, mid points and end points will all look different.

And also, I hope you can still find my words valuable. I hope that they will be relevant, even if our experiences are different. I've done my best to contribute value, ideas and inspiration to a wider community, where I grew up and beyond where I now stand. If you're a single mom taking the bus to work, a PTA mom baking brownies for a bake sale, a financial executive with a nanny and a chef or any other variation of roles and life experiences, I hope you read these words and can feel a connection. I hope you trust your path, and I hope I can support you as you navigate obstacles I could never imagine.

I see you. I believe in you. And I send you love, peace and everything else you need on your journey.

XO,
Lauren

INTRODUCTION

SO...WHO AM I, AND WHY ARE WE HERE?

Have you ever felt like a character in a story someone else was writing? Like somewhere, somehow, you were supposed to go on a quest searching for your true purpose, after which you'd live happily ever after, secure in the knowledge that finally you'd made it to that magical place where every question you'd ever asked yourself was tied up in a pretty little bow?

The process of declaring myself the writer of my own story was really hard because I've come to realize that our stories aren't supposed to have Hollywood-style conclusions.

I have been stuck—like, *really* stuck—so much so that the feeling itself is hard to describe, but I'll try: it's like waking up every morning and instinctively knowing that you should open your eyes. Isn't step one always just opening your eyes?

But they're stuck. They won't open. You're lying in bed, frozen from the inside out. Aware of how your body should be moving but motionless with fear and confusion because you can't seem to just...open your eyes. I've spent a lot of time feeling stuck. Stuck in my marriage, stuck in careers that were unfulfilling, stuck in motherhood. Just stuck.

I love my husband, and I love my kids. I love being his wife and their mom, and I also love doing meaningful work that has an impact on the way I want the world to be. And more often than not, I'm juggling all these things without dropping too many balls. So why have I spent so much time feeling like I was supposed to be doing everything differently?

Probably because for years, I was grading myself according to someone else's standards. I've come to learn and believe that at the end of the day, if you're not centering *your own standards*, you're probably not going to get very good grades.

I was, through a lot of trial and error, able to shift the narrative by taking control of it. I work every day to rewrite what my life is supposed to be—how I'm supposed to parent and love and take care of my people. And I finally realized how perfectly I fit into this world I had created.

Doing this work is the kind of hard that feels like a physical ache with no source—there's no way to soothe or relieve the pain, just move through it. It is perhaps the most challenging thing I've ever done (and I've had three babies!).

Everywhere you look, there are examples of how to live right: smiling faces on social media, perfectly decorated houses, cars that always seem to be shiny and clean, women with impeccable hair and clothing, job titles and careers that seem fascinating and perfect but also a million miles from where you feel you stand. Once upon a time, we'd look at magazines and watch TV shows to see these kinds of women and feel safe in the knowledge that no one was really that perfect. But now, Instagram is a sea of comparisons: if she can do it, why can't I?

It's not like I haven't tried. I loved throwing money at my problems (it was and is so much easier than doing the actual work). I would be certain that each new thing was going to be *the thing* that finally helped me get unstuck. In time, I learned that the only thing you really need to get out of the funk you're in is yourself and the willingness to put in the work. The real work.

I spent so many years stuck because I let other people define my options. I let the expectations of the world define my options, and then when something didn't work out, I felt certain that the problem was me. In reality, the opposite was true: by not centering myself and my own needs (which, if you're a woman and a mom, is strangely still a pretty radical thing to do), I was keeping myself in a box I couldn't figure out how to open.

I should also say that while I now unapologetically make myself a top priority in my life, it's not something I take lightly; putting myself first and being selfish in a way that hurts others are two very different things. Compassion for others doesn't mean abandonment of myself, and care for oneself doesn't mean ignoring the feelings of those around you. Care for myself is care for others because when I'm strong and healthy, happy and confident, I'm a better friend, partner, mom and citizen of the world.

Brené Brown said, "Research tells us that we judge people in areas where we're vulnerable to shame, especially picking folks who are doing worse than we're doing." Remember that next time you feel judged by someone else. Knowing that moving past the vulnerability and struggle, feeling good in who we are and what we're doing changes the energy that we bring to work, life, family and everything else.

No box exists for a former accountant turned doula turned real estate agent turned network marketer who runs a nonprofit, starts a coaching business and writes books...all while driving to endless dance classes and competitions and conventions, learning and growing and raising babies—but that's my box. I built it and continue to build it every single day. I'm not stuck in it; it's a home base where I can explore my thoughts, feelings, wants and needs. It's not set in stone. It can grow, expand and transform through the seasons of my life. It's most definitely not a cage.

I've been in a lot of boxes. I thought I wanted to work in corporate America until I hated that box. I knew I didn't want to be a stay-at-home mom—that was most definitely not my box! I thought I wanted more flexibility in my career, but I didn't know what that meant. I jumped from a pre-fab box to pre-fab box, never pausing to think that it might just be the boxes that were mislabeled, missing some crucial information.

I am, by every metric, so incredibly lucky and privileged in what I have and who I am. But does that mean I have to stop trying to move forward—to design the box meant for me and only me?

We spend so much time looking outside of ourselves, crowdsourcing and desperately asking friends, strangers, Google, Pinterest: What do I want to be when I grow up? Who do I want to be when I grow up? I'm 40, and I still don't feel grown up, let alone have a great answer to that question. What I want to be is *myself*.

I'm not a jerk, but I don't ask for approval. I defined my life based on my values, so I don't feel the need to defend it.

This is a collection of essays about me, but they're not stories that have happy Hollywood endings, because the story of my life—and the stories that come from it—are works-in-progress, just like I am.

ONE
SOBRIETY IS A BOUNDARY
ON QUITTING

BEFORE I STARTED SAYING NO, I was the person who said yes to everything.

I was a good kid, the kind of kid who did what she was supposed to. I grew up poor with a single mom. It forced me to be responsible. Ish. I understood how to make things look good.

In high school, I got a job at a restaurant. I made friends with my coworkers, who were all older than me, and when we were finished with work, we'd go out drinking until the bars closed. We were the late crew.

"I'm spending the night at my friend's house, Mom!"

The food service world is not for 15-year-old girls, but there I was anyway, earning my own money for the very first time.

The restaurant job was my first big lesson in self-sufficiency. I learned that I could have whatever I wanted as long as I was willing to work for it. The way I understood life was like this: if I simply followed a series of logical steps, then I would get my desired outcome and be happy. And if I wasn't happy, then it was my fault.

I took that playbook with me to college, where in addition to excessive drinking and experimenting with drugs, I continued to work hard. I always had at least one part-time job and, during the holidays, I'd work at the restaurant for extra cash (because money didn't just magically appear in my bank account like it did for my friends). Providing for myself was overwhelming sometimes, but I kept reminding myself: you can handle this. Every time I managed to balance my nightlife and come up with the money to provide for myself, it felt good. I'm in control of my life, I thought.

It was logical to major in finance and accounting because I was good at math and had tons of student loans to pay off. Following that decision, I soon noticed that I was falling into a rhythm of crowdsourcing other major life decisions also—all of them, in fact.

"I don't know," I would say, "What do you think?" I asked everyone this question. Did I enjoy the finance world? I never paused to ask myself this question; I just knew I wasn't happy.

I was trying to find my voice, but my voice was always drowned out by everybody else's.

The more desperate I became for guidance, the less discerning I was about where it came from. I felt guilty and then I felt selfish for feeling guilty. In a nutshell, I felt like shit, and when you feel like shit, why not drink excessively?

I wasn't a raging alcoholic living a dismal existence. I didn't lose my car or my house or my children. I was never arrested. I never ended up in the ER. But I was still a sloppy drunk. It was routine for me to wake up in the morning and check my sent messages and my socials with a sense of dread. Had I said anything stupid? Posted anything inappropriate? Who had I run into?

It started to feel exhausting, but I didn't know how to change. Drinking was part of my identity, and yet I was beginning to hate everything about it. I felt uncomfortable in my own skin. I was lost and didn't know what I wanted, sick of waking up with a shame-over, wondering what I'd done the night before.

Before I could cut out alcohol completely, I tried to control it. I made rules. No martinis until dark. A glass of rosé during the day has to have ice in it. Every time I made a new rule, I quickly came up with excuses to break it. Because in the summer, it didn't get dark until nine. Was I really going to wait until nine to have a martini? There was a period of time when I casually did cocaine (a college favorite)—but only on vacation. Still, if the kids went to my mom's house, then wasn't that like a vacation?

Making and breaking my own rules was useless because the problem was not the alcohol. It was me. I couldn't drink like a normal person.

Alcohol made me funny and witty and engaging. It made me a better dancer. It made me outgoing and gregarious. I can so vividly recall my go-to response to someone asking if I wanted a drink; with a big smile on my face, I'd say, "Always!" And I meant it! Rosé with ice was kind of like a seltzer, right?

I spent a year and a half intensely wondering what it would be like not to drink before I stopped. I played out scenarios in my head. What would it be like to go on a vacation? What would it be like to go out to dinner with my friends? How would my life look if I were participating without a drink in my hand?

Before I said no to drinking, I started saying no to other things. No, I realized, I didn't want to be the same kind of mother as others. They loved cooking, and I did not: therefore no, I would not cook unless I had to. I could get takeout instead. And my sister could craft with the kids because she loved crafting and I didn't. Unapologetically, I started outsourcing the things I didn't want to do.

That momentum built up to November 11, 2017, when my husband and I had a bunch of people over, and I drank some champagne. At the time, that meant two bottles—just for me. I felt funny and charming. I woke up the following morning and for whatever reason, this was when I got it. I thought, I am not funny and charming. I'm annoying and a drunk. I am done.

Later that week, I went out to dinner with three friends. They all ordered drinks and I lied to get out of having to. "I've had a headache all day," I said, "I'm not going to drink."

After that, I was like, *Okay, I just had dinner and didn't drink, and it wasn't weird.*

The days kept adding up. I told a friend, "I haven't had a drink in a week and a half, and I think I'm going to stop." My friend didn't care at all about my huge life-changing decision. "That's cool," she said.

That Thanksgiving was the first I'd spent sober since I was probably 12 years old. Afterward, I thought, *Okay, I can successfully not drink during a holiday.*

Then Christmas came. Another holiday sober.

It wasn't until January that I started saying, "I don't drink." Before then, I'd made it sound kind of temporary. "I'm not drinking tonight." I realized that I didn't need to make up excuses about headaches. I didn't need to apologize or explain.

After so many years of wandering around, shamelessly unsure of what to do next, I was defining what I wanted by defining what I didn't want. And after saying no to drinking, I realized I could say no to anything.

I'd been drowning in volunteer duties, so I simply started to decline them.

"Do you make an excuse?" my husband asked me one night.

"I just say no," I replied. As I'd learned, no could be a complete sentence.

On Thanksgiving 2019, I woke up in the morning shame-free and drove to pick up a turkey that had been cooked by somebody else. We had 27 people at our house and not a single dish had been cooked in our oven.

"Must be nice," people have said to me many times. My response to that is yes, it is very nice. I grew up poor and I know exactly how nice it is. I'm not sorry.

Feeling confident enough to do what I want regardless of what other people are doing has given me so much freedom. When I'm listening to my own voice, things seem to unfold in my favor.

I've wanted to be a writer since I was a kid. For the longest time, I'd thought about starting a blog—but I'd always stopped myself somehow with other peoples' opinions. Who would proofread it for me? Who would tell me whatever I'd written was okay? And also, what was the point of a blog? If there was no logical reason to do it, then why do it?

I did it anyway.

After writing my own blog for a few months, I started writing for a mom blog in Westchester County. My post about not drinking got by far the most views of any post I had ever written. Wow, I thought, are that many people really curious about an alcohol-free life?

I imagined that many of my readers were women who lived in Westchester like me. Maybe they were moms who drank rosé, just like I used to. And maybe if I kept putting myself out there, I could help one of those women who wanted to stop.

After I quit drinking, people always came up to me asking me how they could drink less. "I drank a bottle of wine last night," they lamented. "I wish I could do what you do."

I never knew what to tell them exactly. Before I quit drinking, I used to think, I know people in the world don't drink, but where are they? Still, even being that sober person around people who had concerns about their own drinking wasn't necessarily enough. My sobriety was a personal boundary, and you can't set personal boundaries for other people. As nice as that would be, it doesn't work that way. We have to choose sobriety for ourselves, and we have to set boundaries for ourselves. That, in my experience, is the only way to get both sobriety and boundaries to stick.

I never spoke about my sobriety all that often because I didn't think my story was dramatic enough. I didn't have a "traditional" or textbook recovery story. I didn't hit rock bottom, and I didn't have a disastrous story of life crumbling beneath the weight of my addiction. But that's not a part of the necessary criteria to change your drinking habits.

As I started opening my eyes to each aspect of my life, I realized that I didn't have to feel what I thought I was supposed to. I was allowed to stop and ask myself, "Is this really who I want to be?"

As I started enforcing boundaries and stopped apologizing, I saw that I was a person who didn't like herself when she drank. I didn't think not drinking would solve all my problems—if only it were that easy! But I came to believe, slowly and then all at once, that the me who didn't drink might have a better sense of herself than the me who did.

The alternative would have been to wait for a catastrophic event, but why? I didn't need to lose everything to want more for myself. I didn't need to hit a low bottom to create a boundary. I could create my own by saying one simple word: no.

In Glennon Doyle's book *Untamed*, she writes about being afraid of heights because of a simple question: "What if I jump?" The first time I read those words, I felt my entire body relax, and so many of my muddy feelings and thoughts suddenly became clear: I did not trust myself.

Before I got sober, whenever I found myself approaching the edge of some metaphorical cliff in my life, I didn't trust myself not to jump off of it. I could always envision myself doing it and always had to remind myself not to. It was a mindset that kept me from ever walking into a high-stakes situation feeling confident; in the back of my mind, I would hear "Don't jump!" and then, right after, "Why would you jump? Do you want to jump?"

I had peeked over the edge with my heart racing and wide-eyed enough times, and I had to take step after shaky step backward to move forward. Trust, I assured myself. I need to trust myself or I won't trust anything else.

Not drinking is still out of the norm. Most people drink, and it's easy to get caught up in what society expects from us. It's very easy to keep doing what we think we're supposed to. It's very simple to say no, even if it's not all that easy at first—but the good news is that it gets easier and easier.

As I'm still learning, every little time I opt out of living my life according to someone else's expectations, I get a little stronger. My soul believes my own boundaries a little bit more, and gradually, I stop apologizing for them.

Once I got rid of booze and drugs, I started rejecting the influence of certain people, society and my own negative thoughts as well. Anything that muddled my ability to trust myself had to go.

I hadn't hit "rock bottom," I had simply glimpsed a better version of the future and then decided to do the work. And I'm still doing it, one day—and one boundary—at a time.

TWO
SEARCHING FOR THE ONE
ON WORK

"HERE ARE THE MENUS FOR LUNCH," my new boss said. "Let me know what you want—it's usually delivered by noon."

It was the first day of my first post-collegiate job, I had already had four cups of free coffee that day, and now I was getting a free lunch? I almost couldn't believe how far I'd come (ignoring the inconvenient fact that I had $17 in my bank account).

I thought back to me at age six, nearly 20 years earlier, when my mother had to deliver newspapers in the middle of the night to make ends meet. On those evenings, my sister and I curled between stacks of newspapers in the backseat of her car, wrapped in blankets my grandmother and great-grandmother had crocheted for us, looking out the car windows into the darkness beyond.

That memory felt like a million miles away now. Did six-year-old Lauren ever imagine that when she grew up, she would be sitting here, at a desk that probably cost more than any piece of furniture our family had ever owned? My office even had its own door—and a window!

I had graduated and gotten a real grown-up's job—and not as a student or intern but as a full-fledged employee. I was an adult. Now, I was getting my free lunch—one totally different from the ones I once qualified for in school.

I thought I'd stay at that first job for a long time. I thought I'd make a bunch of money and buy a house or an apartment. Or at least a lot of fancy shoes.

The reality was I lasted 11 months and left with an unfortunate realization: I had a college degree that qualified me for a job I fucking hated.

* * *

I worked my first job in 1994. I was 13 years old, and my uncle asked me, "Want to work at the restaurant this weekend? You could be a bus girl!"

I knew whenever my uncle worked at the restaurant he would come home with a pile of cash, so my answer was, "Fuck yeah!"

It was my first real work experience and I loved it.

Almost immediately, I felt confident and competent. I realized I was capable of working hard, running around and being on my feet for 14 hours at a time, which made me proud. On busy nights when orders were coming in, drinks were flowing and everyone was in the zone, it was hard to imagine that any other kind of work existed—even if I knew in the back of my mind that I probably wouldn't work at the restaurant forever.

To this day, "the restaurant" is its own term in my family, and everyone knows what it means. For years, my college friends assumed that my family owned it, since I never called it by its name and so many of my childhood, middle school and high school experiences revolved around the place. We didn't own it, but it felt like it was ours.

I worked there for four years, stopping just before I turned 18 as a freshman in college (though I'd occasionally pick up shifts there when I happened to be home). Through that experience, I had internalized something I thought was important: I loved working. I loved the adrenaline rush of being really, really good at a job. From the coat room to the hostess stand to running the floor as a waitress, I loved to talk and connect with people.

"I moved to this country 37 years ago, and you are the best waitress I've ever had!" a woman who reminded me of my great-grandmother told me on

New Year's Eve 1998, squeezing my wrist a bit. I was home from my first semester of college in Boston for winter break. I tried not to cry as I realized it might have been one of the most meaningful compliments I'd ever received.

I wanted to stay in that warm and cozy moment in the restaurant surrounded by love (and well-tipping customers) forever, especially compared to the uncertainty of my life that was unfolding in Boston. Two days before I left for break, I switched my major to finance. I had student loans to pay off.

* * *

After winter break, I deliberately did not get another job at a restaurant in Boston. While I loved the work, I was, in all my 17-year-old glory, self-aware enough to know that I needed a change. Instead, I paid for my bills, overpriced drinks and even more overpriced textbooks with a mix of retail jobs and paid internships, which had an interesting impact on my wardrobe.

I started working at Ann Taylor when I was 17, and while I didn't really need to buy cashmere sweaters and suits, who was I to argue with 40 percent off? I was a sucker for the employee discount, a fact that followed me to my next job at a hair salon inside Saks Fifth Avenue. Suddenly, it made financial sense for me to pick up my shampoo from Kiehl's instead of CVS.

My internships were paying me more than my friends' were, which only affirmed my decision to switch to finance. It was a logical choice, and after I finished school, the next logical choice seemed to be moving back to New York and getting a job in one of the city's many offices where people did, well, finance and accounting.

I usually don't relate when people talk about how much fun college was. This is not to say that I didn't have fun in college. I did—but it wasn't the carefree kind of fun people often talk about. I wasn't enjoying myself before entering "the real world"; I was already living in the real world and paying my own way.

I stressed about money almost all the time. My finance books were fucking expensive, and I lived in a really expensive city. On top of my classes, I drank a lot, I did drugs and I bought fancy shoes. On some level, the prospect of graduating wasn't filled with dread of becoming an adult. It was actually a relief. It would be the first time in my life that I could have just one job rather than two.

The month after graduation in 2003, a headhunter called and asked if I'd be interested in an accounting job for a private equity firm located just outside the city, in a building I'd actually worked in as an intern in high school. It was one of those moments where it felt like my life—my real life—was about to begin. Armed with my newly minted degree and a few business-casual outfits (thank you, Ann Taylor discount), I was ready to meet a new version of myself.

* * *

As I learned after working as an accountant for a year, sometimes it's easier to know what you don't want than what you do want. I don't want to be an accountant—there, I said it. But I didn't say it out loud, and I definitely didn't say it to the second recruiter I worked with as I explored the option of potentially switching jobs less than a year after graduation.

The longer I was stuck in this job, the more I realized that I could have spared myself a lot of angst if I'd just asked the headhunter about the temperament of the people I'd be working with. My coworkers seemed cranky all the time. They worked strange hours—coming in at or after 10 am and leaving well past 7 pm, which meant that every time I left at 6 pm (when I was actually supposed to be leaving) I got a flurry of snide comments and judgy looks from my frazzled and overwhelmed colleagues. We're booking journal entries here, I thought, not curing cancer and ending poverty. There was free coffee and lunch, but the hidden cost was all the fucking attitude!

I was practically pining for my old office with the expensive desk and window. Now, I was sitting in a cubicle—and not even a real cubicle, but a low, open one where my face was three feet away from someone else's, separated by plexiglass. I had to put up pictures of my friends' kids just so I wouldn't have to stare into the faces of the obnoxious twerps around me who always had something to complain about.

We had a weekly meeting in a glass fishbowl of a conference room in the middle of our office space that, in theory, started at 11 am. The first week I was there, I walked in three minutes before the meeting was supposed to begin so I wouldn't be late. Right away, I was confused about why no one else was walking in.

I sat with a notebook and pen, alone, for more than 20 minutes (I had a hot pink Razr flip phone at the time, which I couldn't amply distract myself with) until finally, the people who were so-busy finally rushed in all harried. As it turned out, their tardiness was not going to be an isolated incident.

Every week, I'd count the people sitting at their desks outside the conference room for 15, 20, 25, sometimes 30 minutes doing nothing while waiting for our meeting to start. I did some math in my head: 20 people wasting 20 minutes of time was over 6.5 hours of wasted time every week! It felt like a power play I wasn't privy to—the busier you were, the more status you had in the eyes of other people in the office. Every time someone walked into that meeting to half-heartedly apologize for being late by saying how busy they were or what a crazy day it had been, what I heard them saying was that their time was more valuable than mine. My wasted time didn't matter because they were so busy.

One day, one of the cranky so busy people sat down next to me in the meeting with a heavy sigh and a stack of papers that landed on the table with a thud. "Ugh, I'm so busy!"

When I'm thinking snarky things, I have the opposite of a poker face. I can't help it. I call it eye snark. It's a gift and a curse, and at that moment, it was raging.

"Me too. And now I just wasted 25 minutes waiting for this meeting to start."

"You should just wait for everyone else to be here before you come in—that's what I do."

In that short exchange, I understood that this was who I would become—the kind of person who was opaque to newcomers, operated on a passive-aggressive timetable and was wrapped up in petty office politics—if I stayed much longer. I knew it was time to once again begin searching for the next job—surely that job would be The One, right?

In the interim, the highlight of my day became making coffee. I loved the moments when the coffee was brewing, and I loved pouring it into my cup and adding just the right amount of milk. I'd go through the ritual twice each morning in the near silence of the office before others started to roll in.

Door slam.

HEAVY SIGH.

Door slam.

HEAVIER SIGH.

I smiled watching the coffee pour from a glass carafe into my cup. I knew what was coming.

DOOR SLAM.

"Why is there never ginger ale in here!?" my boss's boss scoffed as she stormed out of the kitchen.

There's nothing wrong with wanting a cold glass of ginger ale, especially if you're high up on the org chart—but why did she have to yell about it? Why was I suddenly living a life where the presence or absence of ginger ale decided whether or not rage would be tossed around? That energy seeped out like a bad smell and stuck to everything!

As she slung her miserable self out of the kitchen and I resumed my coffee-making process, I sighed peacefully. Job number three, here I come, I thought. I didn't know when I'd actually find a new job—or quit this one—but I knew I was done caring about what happened here.

I realized I was on the absolutely wrong ladder the day a job that would have been a step up became available and rather than accept it, I knew the only way to keep my sanity and happiness was to jump off this fucking ladder as fast as I could. It was time to find another ladder to climb (or sit near, perhaps).

I thought I could naturally shift and course-correct, not knowing yet that what I needed was to be on a completely different road. I assumed it would be like the recalculating sound that pipes through car speakers as the algorithm tries to reroute you when you miss a turn—that some disembodied voice would just tell me what I was supposed to be doing and how I should be doing it. Of course, I didn't think that it might just find me a new route to the same destination.

Now three years post-graduation, I finally found a job that didn't make me miserable. I actually kind of liked it, as it combined my finance background with the chance to actually talk to people like I had in my restaurant days. After working there for almost two years, I went on maternity leave. When I came back, I negotiated a schedule where I worked three and a half days a week. About six months into that arrangement, my boss called me into his office for my annual performance review.

"We really need you to come back full time," he said.

I looked at my watch and glanced out the window toward the daycare center where I'd just been told my nine-month-old was puking. Another perk of my job was its proximity to my daughter Mia's daycare, which in theory was a time saver but in practice meant I spent a lot of time thinking about how strange it was to be so near my baby and yet not able to actually see her. My thoughts went something like: could we hurry this review up so I can go get my baby?

As I thought about it, "part time" felt like an odd way to say I was being paid less to do my same job, just not entirely from the office.

"Okay," I said, taking a deep breath. "I don't want to do that. My last day will be June 15. Also I'm pregnant again, and Mia just puked at daycare, so I need to leave." I offered to stay as long as they needed to transition my work and hire someone new, but once again, I was done. This was perhaps the first time I began to see this secret third option to love or hate, yes or no. This was a great job, but it wasn't for me.

I kept my word. Six months later, June 15, 2009, was my last day of full-time office work, ever. The last day I wore pants with a button to sit in an uncomfortable chair for eight hours. Actually, the chair was kind of amazing—it was the eight hours a day that I couldn't manage.

A few weeks later, on a vacation with my family, I wondered: Is it still called vacation when you don't have a job to go back to? What, exactly am I on vacation from?

I was 28 years old, about to have my second baby and committed to climbing the corporate ladder, but each time I grabbed the next rung, I felt in my bones that I wasn't supposed to be there. As I sat nine months pregnant "on vacation," I asked myself, in no particular order:

What do I want to be when I grow up?

Am I just being too picky? Too particular? Unrealistic?

Is this what the grown-up life I was so eager for is actually all about?

Was it better to be exhausted, overworked, poor and drunk in college?

Should I just be happy with what I have?

They were questions that spun through my mind for years. In reality, none of the jobs I had—even the ones I dreaded going to the most—were all that awful. As time passed, and as I started staring life as a mom of two right in the face, I realized that I actually had it pretty good. It was part of why I resisted believing I could or should want more. I couldn't tap into my gut instinct that my work life should or could be something I really loved as opposed to something I did out of obligation.

It was also the summer of 2009, which most of us likely remember as the time the economy was in free fall—and I'd just left an incredibly secure job with great benefits.

Of course, leaving the world of "work pants" and overpriced (but free) salad lunches didn't mean I was hanging up my hat. How could I? *Look at what you just gave up!* I told myself. *Look at how hard you worked in college and in the years since! What would people think if you didn't accomplish something? Something great!?*

Within reason, I had freedom, support from my family and the opportunity to try new things (within the limitations of breastfeeding, of course). So I started trying stuff out.

In no specific order, I tried direct sales, Pilates instruction, doula work, being a real estate agent, a PTA presidency and co-chairing a gala committee (twice). I took something valuable from each of those paths, but none of them were *my* path.

All the time I was supposed to be "doing it all," I didn't realize that actually meant doing a very specific set of things: getting married, having kids, working a job that seemed impressive and maybe starting a business you referred to in interviews as "like one of my kids, but even more demanding!"

I was a passenger in that process. I was passive as I moved from one job to the next. I took everything as it was, processing it at face value, exactly as it was presented. I assumed everything else was right, and if whatever I experienced didn't fit me, clearly I was the part that was off.

It had been a really big deal to ask for part-time work when I returned to work after Mia was born, but I didn't adequately prepare myself for how to move through it once I was there. I was open to each new job, but at the end of the day, I believed that things were binary. I would either like a job and stay, or I wouldn't, and I would leave. I would be happy, or I wouldn't be. It would be a world in which my answers would be clear and simple, without any fuzzy gray area. I hated that fuzzy gray area.

Of course, I had never had any expectations about the restaurant. I went to work, busted my ass and left with a bunch of money. I never had to put on a show; I was always just me, and so it fit. At the time, I learned that I was good at work, that I belonged in a restaurant-like environment and that it could be an outlet that would keep me away from places I didn't belong (like high school). It took me years before I grasped the real lesson of that experience.

The restaurant had been my happy place. It gave me confidence and a sense of satisfaction so deep that it served as a model for everything else to follow, but it had also come so naturally that I didn't realize how precious that satisfaction really was. I didn't understand the nuance, so I didn't understand the struggles that followed over the next two decades.

I had created a box for "work" and assumed that all aspects of my life that went into that box were things I'd enjoy and be good at. It would be the place I'd thrive, no matter what else was happening around me. It worked in high school, and it worked in college —and then suddenly it didn't quite work anymore. No matter how many times I rechecked that box, it still didn't fit.

I ignored for almost a decade that what I loved most about my earliest jobs were the people. It was the talking and the learning I thrived on—not so much the actual work.

The whole time I was working as an accountant, I would have dreams and vivid memories of my time at the restaurant. The pride I felt, the confidence and satisfaction. I'd find myself staring off into space, giving my wrist a gentle squeeze and remembering the customer who'd reminded me of my great-grandmother. I knew I didn't want to be a waitress, but that feeling, that connection, seemed imprinted in my mind and my soul. I knew the feeling, and none of these corporate jobs provided it.

I went through career after career as an adult recognizing the feeling of being out of alignment but not fully grasping what it was I was trying to re-create and exactly what made me feel so much like me at the restaurant.

The one thing I'd managed to re-create in all the jobs was some combination of a free coffee or free lunch—of course, I had learned the cost was a lot higher than I was willing to pay.

THREE

THROUGH THICK AND THIN

ON MARRIAGE

AS I PREPARED to leave my first post-collegiate job, I walked into the building psyching myself up for what would come next. I took a slow pause before entering the office on that particular morning. I only have to work in this strange building for 10 more days, I thought. There were only two things on my to-do list for the day: the first was to give my notice, and the second was to ask my boss out on a date.

Before you react, I realize what a cliché it is to look for love at the office—and it's certainly not something I planned or even hoped for.

You know how sometimes words sound similar but they're actually really different? Like when people assume that simple and easy are the same? They're not. That's the distinction I like to make when I say that things with Karl and I were quick, but not rushed. Like when you sit down at a restaurant and your favorite meal is right there on the menu: not rushed, but quick because it's perfect for you and makes sense. Yeah, I just compared my husband to seeing the word "truffle" on a menu.

In the months leading up to me asking him out, we'd spent some time together outside of work. A friend from the office who I'd become very close with was moving and she and her husband asked for some help from Karl and two other guys we worked with. Karl and I were each single, the other three married. We helped Kelly and Mike move and a few weeks later, they took us all out to dinner to thank us. There's a visual I'm sure you can picture of the eight of us going out to dinner. Kelly saw it when she asked us to help them with the move. My aunt saw it immediately when I told her who was going to be at the dinner.

We worked in a small office; this wasn't the first time we'd been strategically placed together, and I'm assuming if I'd worked there longer than 11 months, it wouldn't have been the last.

Things were easy with Karl. Conversation flowed. We worked together and you (or at least I) can't be totally on my game for a solid eight hours every day. Also, we worked in the suburbs, which meant that Monday through Friday (sometimes Thursday), these were my people. It was 2003—texting was different, and Facebook wasn't a thing, so connectedness was also different. Whenever I had a thought, the people I worked with got to hear it first. So right off the bat, there wasn't the same mystery there might have been with a stranger or some random guy I'd meet at a bar. I liked that Karl was tall, with a sweet smile and deep dimples, but I also liked that he was even-keeled: it felt like we balanced each other before we were even fully together.

I think we found each other amusing, easy and fun. Our first date was five hours of drinks, dinner and chatting. And then that was kind of it. Another date, and another and another. Sometimes with our work friends, sometimes just us. It all just made sense and felt right and real. He fit into my world with my friends and family, and I fit into his.

I was introduced to Karl on my first day at work: my boss introduced me to him and said, "That's Karl, he's really smart, he knows everything, but don't bother him with stupid questions because everyone does and it's annoying." I was a little intrigued by that comment. Shortly after that, Karl said something stupid or silly in the kitchen; I don't even remember what he said, but I took note...smart and sweet, but not too serious. Definitely not what I'd have taken notice of in college or at a bar... but here, it worked. Here, it felt different.

Karl was the opposite of almost everything else in

my life. He was definitely the opposite of any other romantic interests I had at the time. At 28, he was a full-blown adult with an old soul—something I'm told had been the case for at least two decades prior, if not since the moment he was born. I think it's a first-born thing: my sister is like that, my oldest child is like that, but I am not. And there was something comforting in looking at someone who could balance being a regular person and a responsible adult. It felt hopeful and safe, even if I couldn't name it at first. I walked into his office and asked, fairly certain he'd say yes but still a little nervous. Things progressed from there, and now, almost two decades later, here we are.

Karl told me he was getting his MBA, and I talked about moving into the city and switching jobs. Neither of us could vocalize exactly what we saw in each other, but almost immediately, we knew we were aligned. The conditions might've felt a little wrong, but the connection felt right, so we trusted it and ran with it.

From the start, our relationship was fun and easy, and nobody took anything too seriously. Karl's MBA put him in a world I wasn't fully a part of. For my part, my life in the city with my friends wasn't entirely separate from Karl, but it also didn't revolve around him. We started our relationship understanding that every second of our days wasn't based on one another. We were complements and accents to each other, and neither of us expected—or wanted!—to be a planet revolving around the other person's sun.

We genuinely enjoyed each other for who we were, and we were both flexible, open and interested. We weren't consciously getting more serious, but day by day it became clear that this was what we'd both been waiting for.

When Karl and I moved in together in Westchester, I was a year out from college graduation, overwhelmed with student loan debt and had one credit card that was always one Starbucks latte away from being maxed. All other considerations aside, the decision made sense: Karl's mortgage and maintenance fees on the co-op apartment he owned in Westchester were less than the rent I paid for my sixth-floor walk-up in NYC. Early on, I nervously asked Karl how we were going to split the bills.

"Are you planning on moving out?" he asked. I wasn't. In fact, I fully anticipated that I would only move out of our apartment to move into a house we owned together. "Then why don't you pay your school loans and I'll pay for the house stuff," he said. "It's our financial future so let's look at the big picture, not splitting bills evenly."

It was probably the first time in my life that I felt my overwhelming sense of financial responsibility and dread start to lift. Still, it was a strange thing to hear.

Karl was clearly explaining to me that he didn't want our relationship to be transactional, but I still had a tiny voice in the back of my head wondering if that were even possible.

There's a stereotypical joke everyone has heard—I think it might be some kind of boss-mom urban legend at this point—of a woman who goes shopping at Target (or TJMaxx or Home Goods). She shows up at the register with an overflowing shopping cart, and the cashier casts a sideways glance at her and asks, "Does your husband know about this?" After that, the woman takes the opportunity to lambast the cashier and go on a tirade about how she makes her own money, runs a business and so on.

The cashier's question is atrocious, and its assumptions are bullshit, but I also kind of hate the response; it still preserves the money-power dynamic. What if, instead, the woman's response was, "In my house, we don't use money as a power play. Regardless of whose paycheck fills our bank account, we are a family, and we respect and trust each other enough to spend money without having to ask permission"? It's a nice way of saying, "Mind your fucking business!" (And then afterward, maybe she could give an additional lesson about how not to make assumptions based on strange societal norms from the 1950s.)

From the very beginning, it was clear that Karl

made more money than me—*way* more. I'm not sure he knew he was doing it, but early in our relationship, he made a decision. He liked to eat out, go on vacation and have adventures. Meanwhile, I had debt, and he did not. I could either be the broke girlfriend who always had to say no because I couldn't afford things, or he could pay for the big stuff we did.

There is a funny (and relatable) meme on social media that says something about how having kids was like having a broke best friend who always wanted to do fun things. Of course, in our 2004 reality, I was the broke best friend.

Growing up, I certainly never imagined that I'd be married by 25, and among my cohort there were a few raised eyebrows. Didn't I want to sow my wild oats a bit longer? Have a thrilling affair with a dashing, handsome stranger? Well-meaning or not, I didn't care. I was in love with Karl, and I wasn't going to listen to other people's preconceived notions of how my 20s were "supposed" to go. In fitting with my self-development at the time, my decision was both prudent and not. Karl was definitely "good on paper" and I was in love with him—but I was also 23 and a disastrous drunk.

Karl and I got married on what was (to us) a beautiful Friday evening in June, overlooking the Hudson River. We stood next to each other beneath a trellis that was on the verge of being blown away by the wind and rain. The fact that it was starting to rain was fine—maybe not entirely fine, but also not a big deal considering that we were, you know, pledging to spend the rest of our lives together. Maybe it will wash away some of the beer his cousin spilled on my dress before the ceremony, I thought.

A rainstorm on our wedding day wasn't how things were supposed to go, but we both took it as an invitation. It was raining, but it was still our big, special party, and we were still smiling. It followed that in our marriage, we would make our own rules and execute our own plans in the life we were embarking on together. For us, perfection wouldn't be one fixed vision. Our perfect life was ours to create. I still had about $80,000 in student loans, but it felt less scary than it had. Now, I had a teammate.

Throughout our marriage, I never asked Karl for money. I never had to. If the topic ever came up early on, Karl would put it simply. "The money in our bank account doesn't belong more to me than it does to you," he said. We discussed all big purchases and how they fit into our shared financial picture as a family—but it was never about "earning" the right to spend what was ours.

I never felt like his financial contribution bought him more meaningful input in decisions or gave his opinions more weight than mine. Part of that was because I loved and trusted Karl, and part of it was because he told me so every time he could sense my anxiety. I won't say I never wondered, or worried a little bit, that things might change—but over time, I let my guard down more and more.

I started working as a teenager, and even when I was taking a full course load, I always held down a job (and picked up restaurant shifts whenever I was home). I watched my mom work to support us, and I emulated her in some ways—I was proud to be able to support myself and to be able to buy what I needed (and what I wanted) without having to ask anyone else for permission. When Karl and I got married, and especially when I decided to stay home with the kids full-time, it was an acknowledgment of the fact that we were a team. Karl isn't a dad I have to borrow $20 from to go out with friends—he's my partner, and our relationship is built on the solid foundation we've made together, equally.

From our wedding onward, Karl and I rarely stepped in the same direction at the same time. We never got so far from one another that we couldn't catch up and get back within eyesight or earshot, but it was clear enough that we could both make our own rules without getting stuck on anyone else's path. I had always thought getting married would be the most impactful decision of my life, because it meant choosing a person and growing a family together. What I didn't realize was how much Karl would be the one to help me grow.

When our first child was born and we were in the brand-new baby stage, I assumed I'd take the lead with the day-to-day of parenting. Up until that point, I think Karl had held exactly one newborn, so I was ready to step up and lead. I may have been a little more comfortable with it all initially, but no part of me ever assumed Karl would play the role of backup parent. I knew he was just as willing and capable of caring for our little people as I was, and again, our roles took on their own shapes—ones that looked different than some might've expected.

When our oldest daughter Mia was six months old, I got a call from daycare that she was sick—nothing out of the ordinary, just standard baby-in-daycare stuff. I left work early and picked her up, and the next day Karl stayed home with her. I was newly back to work, having recently finished my maternity leave, and we'd decided to alternate who would stay home on the days daycare was closed or the baby was throwing up or feverish. As I explained the situation to a woman at my office who'd recently had her second baby, she was baffled.

"How does he know what to do?" she asked me. "My husband would never be able to watch the baby all day."

Picture me literally scratching my head at this one. Was there some secret baby-care handbook that only got sent to female caregivers? She was a baby—all you had to do was feed her and smile at her and make sure she wasn't gross. Again: she was a baby. She also wasn't just my baby; she was Karl's baby, too. She was ours, and we were in it together, so it only made sense that I was ready to step up and lead.

My flexible ideas about gender roles came from the fact that I didn't grow up in a traditional house. Things were done by whoever was around. There wasn't an assumption of someone being more qualified or well equipped to do what needed to be done, and there definitely weren't tasks assigned to one person just because they happened to be a certain gender.

If I was sick and needed to stay home or go to the doctor, my uncle would take me. Cupcakes were delivered to my first-grade class by my other uncle who worked at a restaurant—his schedule made it natural for him to take the daytime shift of "adult in charge."

Dinner was cooked by another uncle or my grandfather. It wasn't until after I got married that I started noticing obnoxious commercials for laundry detergent and frozen food—the ones predicated on the assumption that men are idiots and dads are even bigger idiots. I started seeing that there was an entire culture built around the idea of men being unable and unwilling to take care of their own children. That hadn't been my experience as a kid, and that was definitely not going to be my future. In this patriarchal world, the one area that men are deemed less competent is the one that gives them a free pass on the hardest fucking work? Thanks, but absolutely not!

It might sound harsh, but women perpetuate this culture, too! How many times have you heard a mom praise the father of her children for "babysitting?" For showing up at a Girl Scout troop meeting or remembering the name of his kid's orthodontist? How many times have you seen moms "joke" about fathers putting babies in outfits that don't match or in ponytails that look decidedly '80s? If this is ringing at all true, I challenge you to tell me: why does it fucking matter that a baby's onesie matches her sweater? If a baby is dressed appropriately for the weather, isn't that...enough?

I was fortunate that Karl was gifted in the domestic arts, but even if he weren't, our partnership would've still been about pulling your own weight while letting the other person carry what was theirs to carry—and letting them do it their way, without judgment or critique.

I wasn't trying to mold us around some specific vision I had for what we should be. I had no rules or expectations for myself or Karl except to try and keep trying and to stay open. Still, we never sat down to have that conversation necessarily, and we weren't curating our lives. We weren't working toward some idealized picture of what our family would become.

Not long after we had Mia, our son Jacob came along, and a few years later we had Abby, our youngest. Our kids didn't need to be photo ready at any given moment. In another sense, they were always photo ready because I had a phone and could take their picture at any moment, and it had nothing to do with matching outfits and perfectly coordinated pacifiers and accessories. Sometimes their hair was cute, and sometimes it was wild. Karl would often come home from work and ask why the kids didn't have pants on—but they were usually smiling, and that was enough.

As our family grew, we both saw just how nonlinear the growth process was. Raising children and tending to our relationship could not be put on cruise control. Our marriage couldn't be set like a kitchen appliance. We both had restless, independent spirits—at least I did.

Over the years, one conversation became a constant refrain in our house:

Me: "I want to become a doula!"

Karl: "Okay."

Me: "Now maybe I want to try real estate!"

Karl: "Go for it."

Me: "Ooh, what about direct sales?"

Karl: "Sounds interesting…"

My life has always been about course-correcting, shifting and pivoting into the next thing. None of it could've happened without self-trust, but it also couldn't have happened without Karl's endless trust and support. My newest ideas about what I would try next might've occasionally been met with light sarcasm, but one thing Karl never said was "no." We had obvious financial and time limitations as "responsible adults," but he never dismissed any of my ideas, dreams or plans.

"If it's important to you," he would often say, "it's worth our time to talk about it. I believe in you." If anything I tried blew up or turned out to be a disaster, I wasn't met with, "Yeah, I didn't think that would work out." It was always, "So, what's next?"

* * *

Even more than 17 years after our first date, Karl's ability to let me create for myself with support but not necessarily involvement is the ultimate freedom. You be you, and I'm here. In our family and our marriage, nothing has ever been off the table. Everything was open for discussion.

Today, most people know Karl as the one who cooks, takes care of the pool, the dogs, the grocery shopping, the gardening, the baking, the laundry—basically (almost) everything. I like to write, plan vacations and order takeout. I'm a little bit lazy and not a huge fan of spending time outdoors unless a swimming pool and a chaise lounge are involved (hashtag oh, Karl...he didn't know what he was getting himself into with me).

I won't sell myself short; I am good at a lot of things. I know all my kids' schedules and idiosyncrasies. I understand the meaning behind all their different sighs, grunts and facial expressions. I know (usually) what each of them needs at any given moment. I make Karl laugh, and I encourage him to pursue his own hobbies and interests.

My self-belief and trust in who I am took a lot of work, a lot of which I had to do in my own head and on my own time—but that doesn't mean that I did it on an island. As a mom of three, being on an island for extended periods of time wouldn't be super practical (though my schedule is definitely open if anyone has an island they want to invite me to).

At the same time, I never expected marriage or motherhood to become my primary identity. I always assumed I'd still be me while moving into those roles: Lauren, and also a wife; Lauren, and also a mom. That "and also" allowed for flexibility, openness and the option to simply *allow*. I've never expected Karl to take on my journey as his own; he's along for the ride, of course, but I don't need him to believe what I believe. I just need him to believe in me—and part of that means trusting Karl and giving him space to grow into his new roles, too.

Looking back, Karl and I are not the same people we were when we got married, and aside from how well rested we were at the time, I don't ever want to be those people again. Both of us have grown so much, though what has remained constant is that wherever I am and whatever I'm doing, Karl is there, too. Our marriage has centered me in my own life.

Being centered means it's me in all of these roles, but it's also my values, beliefs and needs. Sometimes, I am Karl's wife, my kids' mom and my dogs' backup person when Karl's not around. While those roles turn my attention outward, the center of it all is me, a compassionate person who cares deeply about my friends and family. Of course, I also remember to try and show myself that same respect, care and compassion.

I don't expect to be at the center of Karl's world, and I don't expect anyone else to build their life around me. But there's no one else I'd rather be building my life alongside, one day at a time.

FOUR
ME PLUS THREE
ON MOTHERHOOD

"HEY! How are you? What's new?"

Dread. I hate this question. I hate it because I know what I'm supposed to say, and I'm just so sick of it.

"Great, not much new. The baby is good—she's really such a good baby! I'm back to work part time. I love our day care; it's next to my office!"

Slow down and don't forget to smile.

"I work a half day from home on Tuesdays and I'm off on Fridays!"

Big fake smile.

"It's like the best of both worlds!"

That was painful...why do I even leave my house anymore?

* * *

Karl and I had our first baby in spring 2008. We were approaching our second wedding anniversary, and I was keenly aware of the fact that those three months of maternity leave were the first time in my adult life (since the age of 13) that I wouldn't have to go to work. For some tech context, the iPhone had been around for less than a year. Smartphones and apps and texting weren't anything like they are today. I traded in my hot pink Motorola flip phone for an iPhone just before Mia was born. I don't think I had a laptop at the time, so things like checking email only happened when I was upstairs, sitting in front of the computer in our office. This cool new phone would be a convenient lifeline when I was cut off from the world.

My eyes opened. I was in bed alone. The sound of the grinder in the coffee pot woke me up. I sighed with relief and took a deep breath. She slept through the night. I had just slept through the night!

Whenever my chubby little baby slept later than me, I had fleeting moments where life resembled the one I used to know. With her still sleeping upstairs, I could drink coffee alone while watching *Today*. It was the most normal I felt in months. Seriously: I loved that snoring baby upstairs so much, but also I loved me, and I loved the time I used to spend alone, in the quiet, without explanation or expectation.

I was 27, living in the suburbs and married with a

baby. How had this happened? I'd babysat when I was a tween living in the suburbs with my family, dreaming of the day I'd go off to college and start my cool, grown-up life. I'd hated babysitting, as a matter of fact, and had gotten a job at a restaurant as soon as the opportunity had presented itself. I had never been the kind of kid who fantasized about becoming a mom someday, and yet here I was. A mom.

Five years earlier, I'd been single and going out with my friends in the city on Thursday nights, strolling—maybe schlepping—into my office Friday mornings. I was definitely the only one coming into that office in the same or very similar versions of clothes I'd worn the day before. I was the only one oozing the smell of stale booze. Four years earlier, I'd been engaged and living with my fiancé. Two years earlier, we'd been planning a wedding. A little over a year before, we'd been talking about having a baby.

At the time, we didn't spend too much time thinking about it; we were carefree and enjoyed traveling and going out, but we were also optimistic (or naive) enough not to overthink how a baby might change all of that. In the big picture, we could see what it would look like to add a baby to our family. It was the small moments—the early Friday morning moments—that showed how enormous the space between the old me and the new me had become.

I loved Fridays. I didn't work, but the world did. It was a rebellious freedom where I straddled two worlds, existing fully in neither. I was home all day with a baby on a weekday—but I wasn't a stay-at-home mom. I had a job in the world of finance, but I could watch talk shows all day in my pajamas. I was both, but neither.

Life was good, and it felt like I had everything I wanted. But it didn't feel like it was mine. It felt like I had just ordered a dress online, confident it would be perfect because the model was my same height and weight. Unfortunately when I tore open the package with carefree, optimistic confidence and got dressed, I had to recheck the label because the dress was all wrong. It was supposed to be perfect. What had I done to mess this up?

I'm not being disingenuous when I say I struggled to answer questions like "What's new?" or "How is everything going?" I didn't know what I was supposed to say.

What's new? Literally nothing. Babies are really cute, but they do the same thing every fucking day. Did the people who asked these questions really want to know what was new? I mean, I had a baby; I was home most of the time. Half the people asking had babies of their own, so I knew they knew what living with a new baby was like. A cute little person who didn't speak was who I now spent most of my time with. I had a thousand pictures of her on my phone. She ate a lot, pooped a lot and slept really, really well. I'm a writer and I literally could not think of anything else to say about a happy, healthy new baby.

"It's wonderful," other people would reply to the same questions. "We're so in love, I'm so fulfilled and I just want to be a mom and stay home and do craft projects and stare at this baby all day long."

Was that what I was supposed to say? Because I didn't feel that way. I loved and adored this baby (just like I loved and adored the two others who followed), but I didn't want to do any of the stuff that would have made me a "good" stay-at-home mom. I wasn't suddenly going to start stressing about how to cook Pinterest-worthy dinners (I'm not even sure if Pinterest was around in 2008, but the pressure of it was) or create perfectly curated outfits (for either of us).

I was a walking contradiction. I was supposed to be selfless, only wanting what was best for this baby, and I did. But I didn't just disappear the minute I went from person to parent. I wanted what was best for me, too. And I had absolutely no idea what that was.

Eventually, I did become what other people would probably consider a stay-at-home mom though I never really felt like one, in no small part because Karl and I decided that the kids should still go to daycare even though I wasn't working a traditional job. Dropping them off sometimes felt like navigating a minefield as I looked at other moms and wondered what they thought of me. Were they judging me? Did I care?

The *click click click* of heels rushing down the hall. An extra wave and kiss blown to a baby through a glass door. That used to be me. One slice of work done for the day, now off to the next.

Beneath my feet, I heard the clopping of flip-flops. Jeans, T-shirt, flip-flops. Coffee with a friend, errands, lunch, (nap?) and then back to grab the babies.

Keeping kids in daycare felt like a win for me when it first started. Looking back, it might've been one of the most generous and respectful things that my husband could ever have done for me.

We made the decision that I wouldn't return to a full-time job after the birth of our second baby. Up until then, Karl and I had been splitting the big stuff—if the baby was sick, we'd trade off staying home. But my schedule revolved around daycare drop-off and pick-up and differences in school and work calendars. How did all of these other women do this?! I was constantly bouncing back and forth between me, the woman with a job, and me, the mother with an infant. Dedicated employee who worked hard and strived to overdeliver, in constant conflict with new mother who wanted to snuggle with a baby all the time, in between the endless new tasks I'd been assigned in this realm.

The decision for me to not return to work full time was to alleviate the stress of Karl having to share the responsibilities of taking care of our children (at least in the Monday-Friday, 6am to 7pm hours). But deciding that the kids would stay in daycare part-time was indicative of my belief (and Karl's) that while I'd take on the majority of the childcare responsibilities, it wasn't supposed to be my entire world. At the time, I felt both lucky and like I was a bit of a jerk; none of the other moms wore leggings to drop their kids off at daycare and then went home to watch the news and drink coffee. I now recognize that it might have been one of the most impactful decisions we made. It afforded me time. It gave me quiet. And while I couldn't fully appreciate it at the time, it was setting a foundation for the next decade.

It was a gift to be in my position because it gave me enormous opportunities to try new things. I also felt embarrassed and guilty at first—well, not right at first. At first when I dropped Mia off, I felt amazing. I was eight-and-a-half months pregnant, it was July and I was going home to nap. After that, I had a newborn and a 16-month-old and technically would have been on maternity leave; why would I disrupt my happy little babe's life when she was content with her friends at school? Daycare still made sense. Then, as the leaves began to change and I wasn't going back to my office, I started to feel a strange pressure. Am I doing enough and being enough? I have these gifts—two healthy kids, a loving and supportive husband, time and space and security. Am I wasting them?

These thoughts could have swallowed me if I'd let them. The questions swirling through my head in everything I did eventually became (part of) my catalyst to tune out the noise of the world and start listening to what I thought and felt.

My life as a mom has changed over the years. I think we all somewhat know that as your kids grow, develop and move through different stages of life, what they need from you will similarly evolve. But I've also realized that as I've grown as a person, I've changed as a mom. I don't necessarily think I'm growing in sync or even as a result of my kids' growth, and whether they're correlated or not, there is something interesting and exciting about the assumption that no one has to be static. Minds, ideas, thoughts and priorities can all change. My kids have seen me go through all of these iterations and know that I'm still their mom, but I'm a person outside that role, too. I'm trying new things and looking for new challenges. And I encourage them to do the same.

* * *

My two younger kids dance. I don't mean that they dance around the house or whenever music is playing, but there's some of that, too. I mean classes every day, competitions and conventions most weekends from February to June and me trying to figure out hair bows and makeup and costumes and shoes. It's impossible to say this and not conjure up images of TV dance moms living vicariously through their kids, but I promise that while I'm a dance mom, I'm not a dance mom.

My son Jacob started dancing in the fall of 2013. He was four years old, the middle of my three kids. Maybe if I'd had an interest in (or ability to) dance myself, the moment he started taking hip-hop would have been a bit more momentous, and there'd be some story of how it all began. But I'm not, and there isn't.

When I have to answer the question "How did Jacob start dancing?" I simply smile and shrug. Who really knows?

The likely answer is that someone—probably the babysitter—saw a boys' hip-hop class starting at a local dance studio, and we thought, why not? This could be a fun way to spend an hour.

Never in a million years did anyone think it would end up where it is today. My son and my younger daughter have collected ribbons, trophies and plaques celebrating their success and skill. I know how to make a sleek hair bun. Once I even sewed the straps on ballet shoes, though I swear to myself on a regular basis that I will never do that again.

I remember a friend saying to me at a new mothers' group when my daughter was an infant that she put her child on a horse at a fair once, and it drastically changed the next 15 years of her life.

Sucker, I thought smugly at the time. I was never going to be the kind of mom who let a kid's hobby take over my life. Fast forward to spring 2021, and I realized I could have bought myself a Birkin bag with my kids' dance tuition, so who's the sucker now?

Maybe if I had seen that this were a possibility, there would have been no start at all. Maybe if this were my vision all along, my son would have hated it. When he was four or five, I took my son, my older daughter and two of my friend's high school kids to see Swan Lake at Lincoln Center. If I'd been paying attention, I'd have known right then and there that this boy loves dance. He really, really loves it, and he's good at it. Of my three kids, he's the only one who can stay awake through the *Nutcracker*. So much of who my son is right now revolves around dance—the confidence he has, the people he spends time with, the things he's interested in.

It seems so random for dance to have fallen into our lives, and in a practical sense, it means that we spend a lot of time together in the car while I take them to dance class and competitions. To avoid their faces being glued to their phones all the time, I talk—ramble might be a better word for it—a lot. I tell them about parts of my day, what I did and ate and interesting (or not so interesting) tidbits of what happened in the seven hours they were gone. Sometimes they engage, sometimes they don't; sometimes it starts with funny, interesting or silly conversations, sometimes it doesn't. As an adult, sometimes I'm chatty and sometimes I'm not. I assume my kids have those kinds of days, too.

Above all, I make sure to tell them, in some form, what kinds of things I'm thinking about and interested in. I think kids often have this perception of their parents only existing in the realms where they see them: driving around, making lunches, being parents. I like to round out that image for my kids. If I go out to lunch with my friends, I'll share something about that; if I listen to an interesting podcast, I'll tell them about it. If I read a good book or hear about a new restaurant in town, I let them know.

In part, I want them to know that I'm a real person and that there are many different things I'm interested in and think about. I'm interested in their dance performances, and I love watching them show off new moves, but my thoughts don't revolve around whether or not they're going to nail a pirouette on stage. I want them to have memories of their mom as a person who existed outside of her children. I want them to know that when they grow up, whatever that looks like for them, if they're ever part of a couple or they're parents, that they get to exist as full people, too—outside of any overarching role they hold.

I had three kids in less than four years, all before my 31st birthday. People used to ask me how I managed with so many little kids, and I would answer, completely honestly, "I lowered my expectations."

Cue nervous laughter and an inquisitive look from the person who just posed the question. Did they think I was kidding?

"I'm actually serious!" I would say. "I'm outnumbered, there are so many fucking diapers and I'm not about to let a sink full of dishes be the thing that throws me over the edge."

Not everything is a big deal. You don't have to have

a strong and passionate feeling about everything. Some things should just be able to roll off your shoulders. Also, I'm not just a "regular" parent. I parented through a fucking pandemic. Every parent who's kept it even halfway together since March 2020 deserves a fucking medal because "global pandemic" was most definitely not mentioned in any of the parenting books I've read. (Actually, I've never read any parenting books, but I'm assuming that they don't cover such lessons.) The pandemic, as I'm optimistically writing about in the past tense (or at least as a winding down event), brought out a lot in a lot of people—some good, some bad, some expected and some seemingly out of nowhere.

In summer 2020, there was a lot of "processing out loud" on the internet. There was uncertainty, debate, discussion and endless speculation about what school would look like in the fall. It was about what all aspects of life might look like, but it felt especially pronounced around kids and school. I won't rehash any details or opinions about schools, masks or anything like that. But there was one concept that kept popping up, and I had a big, big problem with it. In many ways, it felt like it was incredibly clarifying about who I was as a mother, how I viewed that role and what values I set for myself and my family. I'm talking about the idea that kids shouldn't see their parents struggle—with feelings, with stress, with anything.

I want my kids to be happy. Not like buy-you-a-car-and-video-games-so-you're-happy, but like deep down contentment. Inner peace. I want to raise children who grow up knowing that inner peace is possible. Children who become adults and understand when they're out of alignment, when they've lost that inner peace, when they need to course-correct and when things are off. If I don't let them feel the good and the bad as kids, or if I try to narrate their feelings for them, they will never know what it means to feel their feelings and they'll never understand how to trust them.

I've seen so many Instagram posts about making this time less scary for kids, and I get it. I don't want my kids to be afraid of the world even though it's filled with a ton of objectively scary shit. But I also don't want them to pretend like everything is okay when it's not, which means I have to give myself space to feel that, too.

Children are people. They're learning to be adults, and they're learning to process and wade through heavy stuff. I'm teaching my kids to be people in this strange world, and they're learning about what kind of people they want to be—not who I want them to be. That's what I want them to hold close as they grow up and begin grown-up lives of their own. That my being devoted to them—and I am—and loving them—and I do—doesn't mean I'll only love a certain version of them. Dance might not have been an activity I'd have chosen for them to be passionate about, but it's what they are passionate about, and the fact that they care about it so much—that they care about anything this much—is evidence that I'm on the right track.

As they grow up, there are a lot of things I want them to remember—family holidays and vacations, carnivals and parties and all kinds of fun things. But I also want them to remember the times that weren't so good. The days that were hard and sad and scary. I want them to know and understand the whole array of feelings, trust them, and know that they're okay. I want them to remember riding in the car, talking to each other and to me and their dad. I want them to remember everything.

FIVE
A FEW WORDS ON A BAD WORD
ON "SHOULD"

I WANTED TO BE A WRITER—LIKE, from the time that I was five. I knew somewhere in my five-year-old heart that putting words onto paper and having other people read those words was my destiny.

In third grade, I wrote a book report on the pioneering female journalist Nellie Bly and then became convinced that I'd grow up and be just like her, traveling the world and reporting on what I saw in far-flung locations, changing the hearts and minds of people at home who would wait with bated breath for my next dispatch. Watching *Murphy Brown*, a sitcom about a woman who took pride and pleasure in her work as a journalist, fueled this dream. The part where she's an unashamed, recovered alcoholic might have been a bit of foreshadowing of what was to come.

Filled with excitement for what I was sure was the

beginning of a long and impressive writing career, in 1989 I put a word processor at the top of my Christmas list. The morning came, and there it was under the tree—and I thought my head would explode with excitement. If you're under the age of 40, imagine a fancy typewriter or primitive computer. If you're under the age of 30 and don't know what a typewriter is, think about a printer that prints one letter at a time immediately after you type it...yeah, I hear how this sounds.

You might soon discover (or perhaps you've already guessed): I don't like being told what to do. The idea that my new friend Nellie Bly was told "women aren't reporters" was stupid to me and definitely a fight I knew I was meant to carry on.

What intrigued me about these women, Nellie Bly and then Murphy Brown, was the way they thought. It sparked an overwhelming desire to think and write and ponder—and write some more.

And then, eventually, I got to college. Where, for better or for worse, it became clear that I was good enough at math to understand the reality of my student loans. I was also good enough at math to understand that a career in finance—not the kind of thing third grade me would have been excited about—would, also for better or for worse, be one that I'd likely be good at. It would be, above all, a logical choice. If I took a poll, people would approve. And in my mind, I was always polling the crowd.

Writing was not a poor kid's career path. I don't know if anyone ever specifically said that to me, but I felt it. Right now, 23 years after first choosing a major and deciding which classes I'd take as a freshman in college, I can clearly see that those words were a lie built on fear.

But at the time, and without the ability to say, "Hey Siri, can I make any money as a writer?" it felt like the only truth. There was no Twitter, no online writing community I could tap into for advice, guidance or commiseration. It would be years before I even owned my own computer. This was my reality.

I remember being at a bar with a bunch of people I worked with in finance in Boston. I was still in college, and boozily contemplating a move back to New York after graduation—or at some point in the coming years. One of my colleagues said, in a serious and interested way but definitely with a lighthearted spirit, "What do you really want to do?"

It was like a water balloon had been thrown at my face and burst open. The tears just exploded out of my eyes as I sobbed, "I just want to be a writer!"

Look of horror. Silence. Eyes blinking. A few more seconds of silence. We were friendly enough (and, by this point in the evening, boozy enough) that he didn't simply run away, though that would have been a perfectly acceptable option. I genuinely think he was shocked. It seems a simple enough question: if that's what you want to do, why don't you do it?

I don't know. That was part of the answer. The other part, the one that felt most pressing to me at the time, was that I was about to have a degree in finance and accounting, and $80,000 in student loan debt. I also don't think you're supposed to make career changes before you even graduate, or when you're this close to graduating. I had spent my college years studying, partying and working, and while the version of me that was a writer never stopped existing, I had kind of stopped feeding her. I didn't have clips from the school newspaper, or essays and poems that had won department prizes.

What I did have was a résumé that would have impressed hiring managers at big, fancy banks and financial companies.

I graduated from college, moved to New York and got a job in finance. Just like I was supposed to. The minute I sat down in my fancy office chair and looked out my big office window, it hit me: I had done a damn good job painting this picture, and I had done a damn good job selling it to everyone, including myself.

I also had my own imagination and my own willpower. I worked retroactively, creating a new version of myself—not the 21st-century Nellie Bly or the Murphy Brown of the new millennium, but a me who wore a power suit and looked out of my big window in my big corner office at some fancy finance firm. That picture was now my definition of success. How did a struggling writer fit into the mix? How could a struggling writer compete with the image I knew was within my grasp? Why was it that I could only imagine my life as a writer to be one filled with struggle? I'd gone without, I knew what it meant to struggle and stress about paying bills. I like expensive shoes, and I used to like expensive cocktails at fancy clubs (they've since been replaced by expensive espresso drinks at my favorite coffee shops). A big, reliable paycheck felt safe. It felt like the pathway to fun. I didn't yet understand the power behind those words.

Look: I'm not one for being prim and proper when it comes to word choice—that's a polite way of saying that on a daily basis, more than one "bad" word comes out of my mouth, and I don't feel bad about it one bit. There is, however, one word that does truly make me shudder: the dirty "s" word...should.

Carrie Bradshaw (my least favorite *Sex and the City* character, in case you were wondering, but one that's often hard to escape if you're a woman of a certain age with literary aspirations) first attempted to dismantle this on her old-school Mac in the early

2000s. Her trademark "writing face" on, sitting in front of an open window in an apartment there's no way anyone could afford on a humble columnist's salary (I know, I know—it was rent controlled…but she wrote a weekly column in a weekly newspaper). We saw that flashing of the cursor as she typed, "Why are we should-ing all over ourselves?"

Carrie may have spouted plenty of nonsense in her day, but let's give credit where credit's due: why do so many smart, kind, caring, incredible women have the life sucked out of them by people, places and things they should love? In my case, it was because I was afraid. Afraid of what might happen if I was honest about what I really wanted to do with my life, and afraid that even if I tried, it might not work for me.

What would a course correction—a transformation into the writer I wanted to be—have looked like for me during the years I spent pretending like I had it all figured out? As much as it pains me to type these words, I have to be true to my post-college self and tell you that whenever I questioned the choices I'd made, I wondered: what would people think?

* * *

I didn't stop writing; I just didn't do it in any way that would let people know. I wrote for myself because that's where it seemed safe. That's where it was logical. A few years ago, I was cleaning out old boxes from my closet and came upon a floppy disk (my kids have never seen one before and said it looked like someone 3D printed the "save" icon) with the words "Porté March 2003."

My maiden name. My first attempt to write a book. Hidden away in the technology equivalent of a lock with no key. I thought about that floppy disk on the first day of a writing workshop I signed up for.

"So," the instructor asked. "Why do you want to start a blog?"

It seemed like a simple enough question. The women before me had answered with ease, and the words seemed to flow effortlessly from their mouths.

One by one, as they answered, I could feel my palms getting sweaty. Fuck, maybe I shouldn't have come to this class. Intently listening, judging myself and admiring the confident answers I heard, I wished I could disappear. I wished, more than anything, that I had stayed home. As much as I willed it not to, my turn arrived.

"I don't know," I said. "I just really like writing and always have."

It felt like there was a screeching halt to the conversation. No one added anything, and there wasn't much more to say than that. Next.

For the next three hours, my mind wandered through a field of logical, rational reasons why a person might start a blog. Why I might start a blog. Feeling fully inadequate and out of my element, I judged every possible answer. I questioned my worthiness, my abilities, my commitment.

Fifteen months later, in a room full of women who could have been strangers but whom I felt closer to and more relaxed with than most people in my life, the same question was posed. This time it didn't feel like an inquisition, although in fairness, the first time it wasn't either—we were doing introductions at a Starting Your Blog workshop, so it probably made sense for the instructor to ask. All the feelings of judgment were entirely created by insecurities.

"I want to write. I love to write! And I think someone might feel seen and heard and appreciated by my words," I said, every fiber of my being relaxed as I spoke. This was the day that I would commit to starting my blog—and thus to writing and putting words out into the world. This was the day that I realized I didn't need a reason, I didn't need a goal, I didn't have to draw a logical line from here to there to justify a thing I was going to do. I gave myself permission to do the thing and see what happened.

It was a shift in justification, in perception of myself and how to derive value. A shift in explaining and rationalizing. It was a step in telling the "should" part of my brain to knock it off—that I was in charge now.

I also had, at this point, enough life experience to know that if I wanted to write, I had to make time for it. No one was going to ask me to start writing again. I had to do that. I had to decide. I had to remove all of the things that made it so much easier to not do the thing I wanted to do. I had to tune out the words I assumed others would say, and I had to soothe the part of me that was terrified to actually move forward.

I felt something shift. I didn't know what it was, but it felt important—and necessary. It felt like it should be documented and written—and shared!

I did start a blog, and I did force myself to sit down and write even when I wanted to do literally anything else. I write and have written about a little of everything there, from drinking (and not drinking) to parenting to real estate to Instagram. It's a place where I can work out my thoughts and ideas in real time, and it's a place where I can write the stories I want to read. Sometimes I illustrate posts with pictures of my kids, and sometimes I talk about places I've been or people I've met. Writing, for me.

I had the space and the time and the ability. I could say I didn't have time or that I was too busy, but that wasn't true. What was true was that it was safe and easy and comfortable to watch reruns of my favorite shows or to spend a day binge-watching HGTV. I was out of excuses, so I started to make some small exchanges: instead of watching *The Real Housewives of New York* and rolling my eyes at the antics of Bethenny Frankel and company, I would use one hour —equivalent to one episode of TV—each day to write. This had the added bonus of weaning me off programs that added no value to my life. And while I can't say I don't still check in on my favorite reality characters, I can say that writing gives me something they never could.

SIX

MY BEST WORST FRIEND

OR, THE STORY OF WHEN I MET A NARCISSIST

WHEN I LEFT the corporate world, I found myself in transition. Even though I had felt antsy and unsatisfied at work before, it was also safe and comfortable. Even if I'd been faking it a bit, I was faking it in a way that came very easily to me. On top of it all, I was also moving from married-with-no-kids Lauren to mom-of-two Lauren.

I was plunging into possibility, waving goodbye to the safe shores I'd known and felt comfortable on and looking for something amazing and new—and then I met Sarah.

I'd just had my oldest daughter when I met Sarah at a baby play group. Something about her energy was magnetic. The confidence in her petite frame and bohemian style. A whimsical and effortless flow of her long, blonde beachy waves. People wanted to stand next to her except for those who didn't, and I'd look at them with a strange contempt. They must just be intimidated, I'd think. This also had the effect of drawing me closer to her. I didn't think of myself as someone easily intimidated or pushed around, so the fact that I could hang with Sarah must have meant I had something other people didn't.

She was a doula, and everything about her work intrigued me. I thought maybe it was a path that might be right for me, and Sarah was ready and willing to become my mentor, confidant and friend. Very quickly, it felt like aside from my husband, she was the person I spent the most time with.

It is astonishing to see how tried and true the narcissistic playbook—of which Sarah was an excellent student—really is. She love-bombed me, making me feel like I was, above all else, so lucky to have her in my life. Other people "couldn't handle" the way she told it like it was, but I could, she said—and that made me special. She began to take up more and more space, and I eagerly made room for her. I had so many questions; she had all the answers. I somehow felt like my proximity to her was necessary in not feeling quite so lost and confused.

It shifted the narrative in my head from "there are so many questions and no answers" to "someone else has the answers and I need them to tell me!" It changed the way I thought about each situation and scenario as I navigated through this new phase of life. Instead of wondering about things, I wondered what I should be thinking about them. I looked around to understand how I was supposed to feel instead of tapping into my own actual feelings. Something was off, I could feel it, but I was deeply immersed in not feeling—so I asked, and the answers all seemed to point to me and the many ways in which I was not measuring up.

Sarah began to take up more and more space, finding subtle ways to tie my life to hers and to keep me in a space of feeling like she knew everything I didn't. So many questions, and she had all the answers. Throughout our relationship, I alternated between feeling desperate for her approval and support and feeling like I'd won the lottery to actually have someone like her there to encourage me and to fix all of these things that were so obviously wrong.

My first clue that something wasn't quite right should have been my constant need for approval from just one person: Sarah. It was nothing anyone else would have noticed, but the feelings I had—like I was disappointing her, like I was failing myself—were very real. One afternoon, we were giving a presentation to a few colleagues. Actually, it was my presentation, but somehow it became ours. It was just a regular Tuesday afternoon, and yet in the world I was living (or floundering) in, it felt like my chance to prove myself—to her and to everyone else. This was the moment that I would be impressive.

As we sat in the conference room chatting and waiting for everyone else to arrive, I felt confident. I knew what I was going to say, I was excited and comfortable. I was ready!

The door opened and we glanced over from our conversation. A colleague poked her head in and said, "I'm going to grab a glass of water—need anything from the kitchen?" and then bounced down the hall. I closed my eyes, took a deep breath and reminded myself that I was ready. It was almost time.

As I exhaled and opened my eyes, quietly rehearsing the words I was going to speak to the group, I noticed that Sarah was staring at me with a look on her face that suggested concern.

"Were you just asking a question?"

Huh.

"What do you mean?"

"Sometimes it sounds like you add a question mark to the end of sentences, like you're asking a question. Do you do that on purpose? It makes you sound unsure of yourself. Do you hear it?" Her eyes were sympathetic, concerned. Her voice was assertive. Her body language was exuding power.

My mouth was suddenly dry.

"What? No, I...No, I wasn't asking a question?"

Wait, had I actually just done it? Wait, what? That was a question, but before that, it wasn't. Was it? Eyes blinking and mind racing, I had a for-real question I'm still asking almost a decade later: what the actual fuck?

Twenty minutes later, I was mid-presentation, speaking as if my words were being played back through a voice altering machine. I paid extra attention to my emphasis and intonation. Did that sound like a question? Was that said with authority? Did I sound weak? Was I asking permission? What the fuck am I even talking about?

The meeting ended, we said our goodbyes and as we gathered our bags, Sarah glanced over at me and asked, "So how do you think you did?"

I took a deep breath. Don't ask a question, I thought. Answer with confidence.

"I don't know—a seven, maybe?"

Fuck, I said it like a question.

"I would have said a six," she said. "There's some work to do, but I can probably help." Her faux-concern felt like a life vest and a slap in the face.

"Thanks?" I replied.

* * *

Soon, everything coming out of my mouth was wrong and Sarah was ready to fact-check. Every question I asked, she had the answer.

I can recognize now that she was trying to destabilize me. It worked. I was wobbly, shaky and unsure in every step I took. I'd gotten to a place where I couldn't make a single decision without her weighing in. Then, when she'd deign to do so, she'd gain a little more power over me.

I said, "I made an appointment to see a therapist."

She said, "Oh, well, I guess if you think you have issues that I can't help you with, then go for it."

I said, "I love vacation!"

She said, "It's so strange that you'd go four days without talking to your kids."

I said, "We had the best cupcakes last night."

She said, "Oh, I guess you didn't mean it when you said you wanted to lose weight."

I said, "I keep forgetting all this stuff I need to do to get Mia ready for kindergarten."

She said, "That's so strange, you remember everything! I wonder why you're so disinterested in your child's life?"

I said, "I just don't want to be the mom who bakes and leads Girl Scout troops. I don't want to be the class mom."

She said, "I guess some people just love their kids differently."

I said, "I don't like tumultuous relationships."

She said, "I'm sorry your marriage doesn't have the same passion as mine."

I said, "I have plans with other friends."

She said, "Are they really your friends?"

* * *

I struggled as a new mother in the ways I imagine many new mothers struggle. Not in the mothering part necessarily, but as still being a woman while also being a mother. Being a mom and taking care of a new little person came very, very easily—it was almost shocking. At the same time, I was watching Karl become a dad, and I loved the new version of our family that was beginning to take shape.

What I wasn't so great at? Being myself.

Figuring out how to balance my life as a mom with everything else I already was—that threw me for a loop. Up until that point, I was me. I worked, I felt accomplished and I felt smart. I was proud of myself and excited to tackle new challenges and stages of life head-on. But as a mother, I felt like I was in purgatory: not fully in one place or another.

I hadn't imagined being an accountant as a little

girl or a teenager, but I hadn't imagined being a mom in the suburbs, either. I knew no one's life turned out exactly as they imagined it, but I felt like I'd gotten off the freeway an exit early and ended up in a whole other dimension. Things weren't bad; they were actually (annoyingly) kind of great. I might not have been able to articulate precisely what I felt like I was missing, but there was definitely something. When I got to know Sarah, I thought that she might hold the missing puzzle piece.

When I started having kids, my world shifted a bit. I maintained parts of myself and things I enjoyed, but it always felt like I was stepping out of one role to spend time in another. Leave my kids and husband at home to go out with my friends in the city. Miss a party or event because I was doing mom stuff. I had some other friends with kids, but I still felt like I was on my own little island, not really belonging anywhere.

I longed for the old me. This was exacerbated by the fact that for the past 15 years of my life, being a worker and employee had been at the center of my identity. Suddenly that felt ancillary, like my job was no longer a source of my esteem and worth—and it made me wonder where my value actually came from now. I knew objectively that keeping my kids alive and happy every day was an accomplishment, but changing diapers is changing diapers—once you get the hang of it, it's pretty much the same each time.

Feeding the kids, putting them down for naps, reading to them—I loved doing all of those things, but they didn't exactly require a ton of critical thinking skills. It felt like the world was telling me that my new value, identity and worth should be (or was) enmeshed in the mom title. The thought of that felt like I was suffocating in an itchy, ill-fitting wool sweater on a hot summer day.

I didn't—and don't—want motherhood to be an all-encompassing title or role, in part because I don't ever want my kids to feel like their main role in life is being my child. I didn't realize it at the time, but I was trying to navigate and name something that would be so big and profound and impactful on the rest of my life. It felt like I was rejecting something the world was expecting of me, but really it was one of the few times that I truly set up a boundary around what fit and what didn't for who I was and who I was trying to become.

I am a writer and also a mom.

I am an entrepreneur and also a mom.

I am a coach and also a mom.

I am a woman, wife, friend and also a mom.

The "mom" title isn't the center of who I am; Lauren the person is, even if I struggled with it for so long. As I took those first steps into my new role, leaving the hospital as a new mother just two weeks shy of my 27th birthday, I still felt like I should be me and also a mom—but I didn't know how. What's more, I didn't see a lot of representation of myself out in the world. I know now that many people feel this way when they become parents.

Sarah's life was a whole new mental category for me. It seemed like a bridge from where I was to where I wanted to go, and our relationship quickly went from professional to personal to familial.

After she established herself as my professional mentor, she swiftly shifted into my personal life coach as well. She created a space where I felt like I could remain essentially myself in a way I'd been craving ever since becoming a mom. And to be clear, I made room for this. I felt like I needed her and created the space for this dynamic to fuel me.

Sarah filled a void, and at first it was with love; isn't that how these things always go? She wanted to be my best friend and my mentor, my work wife and travel buddy. She wanted to have our families get together for dinners on Friday nights. She had opinions about everything, and since hers was always the loudest in any room, I didn't even notice, at first, that her voice was beginning to replace my own.

During my time as a doula, I went into homes and lives during intensely intimate moments, trying to strike a balance between imparting what I knew, providing what was needed and letting new families work out their own way of doing things. This put me in the path of all kinds of people and all kinds of new fathers. Men who didn't want to change diapers and men who thought no one without an engineering degree could actually change a diaper correctly. Yeah, dude, you have a Master's from MIT, but your swaddle skills still suck. Some men thought I was essentially a very expensive maid, there to ensure their sleep wouldn't be disturbed by a crying baby and their wife wouldn't be too tired to put dinner on the table.

One thing I learned very quickly in my doula career is that I am deeply and profoundly uncomfortable around controlling men. I didn't grow up with controlling men in my life. After my parents split up, my mom, sister and I moved in with extended family. My uncles and grandfather, who were always around, were men who cooked and cleaned and spent time with kids without calling it "babysitting."

I remember working with a client relatively early in my doula work and being so uncomfortable around her husband; throughout our prenatal meetings and all through her birth, I couldn't quite figure it out. About a week after her birth, I spent an evening working with them and helping with their new baby. Red flags and loud warning bells filled my head the entire time. I didn't want to be there, and I felt it in every fiber of my being.

That evening, the three of us, along with their newborn, ate dinner together. I come from a big Italian family and believe it's a lovely gesture any time you're included in a meal, since feeding someone is the ultimate sign of care and love. So I happily accepted. The baby was a bit fussy, so I held him to make sure the new parents could enjoy their meal. With a baby in my arms and a plate of food in front me, the husband poured the contents of an entire bottle of wine equally into three glasses for himself, his wife and me.

As he started to pour my glass, I looked up and said, "No thank you, I don't drink while I'm working."

Still pouring and without making eye contact, he responded, "Well, I'm paying you and I say it's okay."

If I were an animal in the wild, every hair on my body would have been standing upright. Head cocked to the side, restrained half smile on my face as I slid the glass of wine away from my place setting, I repeated, "I don't drink while I'm working."

He made eye contact then. My eyes said, in no uncertain terms, don't fuck with me while my mouth said, "but thank you anyway."

I left their house a few hours later, driving down their long dirt driveway and through winding country roads, and arrived home with an even deeper appreciation for my husband and the relationship we'd built. I was happy to never return to that house again, and happy that my life was one in which adults treated each other with respect.

Countless times over my nearly 14 years as a parent, my kids and I have left situations where I've said things like, "So, what Bob did was fucked up. We don't behave like that—it's not cool!" My kids can almost anticipate it. We'll get into the car and they'll say, "We know—they were a jerk and we shouldn't do that." Damn straight! But that's now. For a long time, I was so hyper-aware of the way men treated women that I missed other big red warning signs. I felt safe in the knowledge that I would never let a man treat me like that!

You know who did treat me like that? Over and over and over? Sarah.

* * *

Over time, it felt like I was changing. It felt like growth, like I was moving in a direction and becoming something more and different. It felt like I was stepping into who I was supposed to be... sort of. Life looked rosier than ever—from the outside. I was working and felt accomplished in a career I thought I loved. I had friends I thought were amazing. I had a supportive husband and cute kids who slept through the night. I'd lost the baby weight...I was living the dream. Ha. The fucking dream. Increasingly, it was more like a nightmare.

I was a disaster—slowly at first, but then *bam*, I was fucking in it! I was judging myself against standards and ideals that weren't mine. I had been shown a picture of what it meant to be a boss, a mom, a wife, a woman, a mother and a friend; I assumed every step that didn't put me closer to that image was wrong.

More and more, I found myself asking questions like, "Should I be upset about that?"

Today, I can't imagine being so disconnected from my own feelings that I would look to someone else to ascertain how I might be feeling. But what I thought I should feel and what I actually felt were different, so clearly something was off. I assumed it was me.

"I don't know...."

"I don't know...."

"I don't know...."

I said and thought this over and over and over. It was an excuse, it was a deflection, it was avoidance, and it was a big fucking lie.

They were the words that emerged when I had to say something, but what I felt and what I thought I should feel were at odds. As the distance between external and internal grew greater and greater, parts of me and who I was started to get lost. I wasn't confident, I wasn't funny and I wasn't happy. I wasn't me, and it was exhausting. My true feelings were being kept at bay, and the only feelings I had were the feelings Sarah (or the world at large—which felt like the same thing at the time) had about me.

The truth was, every time I said, "I don't know," I did know. Even so, so much of my life was wrapped up in all of the shoulds, in the image of what I thought I was supposed to think and feel and look like and how I thought I was supposed to behave and believe, that I was afraid of what knowing who I was and what I wanted would do to me. I had gotten so far away from the real Lauren.

And then one day, the dam broke. All the feelings I'd been stifling all fell out of my mouth, and with each word, I felt more and more connected to what I was feeling and who I really was. I'd been seeing my therapist regularly for about six months when I felt ready to say the words I had been afraid to even think for so long:

"Sarah is a bad friend, she is not 'my person' and I want her out of my life."

Each word flooded into the strange world she and I had created and washed away my self-doubt. They washed away the distance between what I felt and what I said, and they broke Sarah's hold on me. I started telling her that she didn't know what was best for me—not just because she didn't know but because she didn't want what was best for me. She wanted a broken Lauren she could constantly dangle carrots in front of, keeping me on the hook for more. She didn't want me happy and thriving and confident because happy and thriving and confident Lauren would have told her to go fuck herself.

I recommitted to being me, and I worked on extricating myself from the twisted world that we'd created. It wasn't real, but I had also put so much time and energy and sweat into it. I knew the only way to save myself was to walk away. Sarah wanted to win; I wanted peace. For a variety of reasons, some of them legal, I won't get into the particulars; but I will say that, in general, narcissists all have the same bag of tricks, and all of them think they're smarter than everyone else. In reality, they rarely are.

It was a process—physical at first and then emotional. I needed to no longer be in this world I'd created. But the feelings about making that move were far less clear, less straightforward. What did the happy times in the not-real reality mean? These conflicting emotions seemed to be mutually exclusive, and yet there they were: both real, both felt, both confusing. The physical aspect was so much easier to make sense of. The emotional side of moving past this relationship meant coming to terms with all the fuzzy parts.

After cutting our personal and professional ties, I started figuring out what my life was going to look like without Sarah. Seven years later, early in 2021, I took a couple of workshops with the amazing Jen Pastiloff—writer, yoga instructor and extraordinary human being. Part of the workshops dove into confronting our "inner asshole" (side note: if you haven't read her first book, *On Being Human*, I highly recommend it).

My inner asshole is the voice in my head who reminds me of the things this person tried to instill in me. My inner asshole is the remnants this woman left in my head—and to be completely clear and fair about myself, I let this voice in. I welcomed and made room for it.

But my own voice, every day, gets louder and louder, and I know that someday, I won't be able to remember what hers sounds like. I want to share some of the words I wrote to my inner asshole:

Dear Inner Asshole,

I see your game. You've shamed me into thinking this is reality, but it's not. It's a game. And I am not playing anymore.

The game where you let me see what I can have, what I want and what I dream of, and then make it out of reach. Make me feel unworthy of it, unqualified and undeserving. Guilty for even thinking I should want it. You made me beg, but it was mine all along.

I'm not playing your game.

You made me doubt myself...

You shook my trust...

You isolated me with fear...

You've overstayed your welcome.

Thank you for forcing me to do this work. Thank you for making me realize just how capable and worthy I am. Fighting against you, fighting for me has restored my trust in myself more than I ever thought was possible.

I get it. I asked what was wrong with me. And you told me...a lot. And now, I'm not asking anymore.

I know what's right with me. I have the answers I need. You helped me find that. I've repaired the damage.

I've got this. I'm sure you'll want to take credit for what I've accomplished...and I won't fight you on this. I choose peace over being right. I choose peace over your voice. I choose peace and I choose myself.

Fuck you.

Thank you.

But I don't need you anymore.

* * *

My years with Sarah were a crash course in so many of the most important lessons I've ever learned—about people, relationships, expectations and myself. When I write "thank you," I mean it. When I write "but I don't need you anymore," I really mean it.

Talking about it is unsettling. When I think about sharing the story of me and Sarah, my first instinct is to shout, "Fuck no! I sound like a whiny, needy, insecure idiot!" But I wasn't. My next thought is, I'm over this! I've moved on and I don't need to go back there. And that's true; I am, I have and I don't. But the lessons I've learned and the resilience I've found, the person I've become and the awareness it has created, shouldn't be mine alone. I know there are so many people struggling through these kinds of relationships, questioning everything about who they are, what they want and where they're going.

Two weeks after my relationship with Sarah imploded, Karl and I went to Vegas. We'd had a long weekend trip planned for a while, and I think he was happy to have a reason to get me up off the couch and out of pajamas, which is where I was physically and mentally after everything ended.

My mind was swirling with questions and scenarios, with sadness, rage and shame. Nothing had been real in that relationship. Well, not exactly nothing—my feelings were real, but they were feelings about situations that weren't. It had all been a game, a big joke that I wasn't in on. Towards the end of our relationship, as the wheels were starting to come off the bus, I'd have moments of feeling like Jim Carrey's character at the end of *The Truman Show*, standing in the middle of a made-up rainstorm, soaking wet, desperate and screaming.

Is that all you've got!?

By that point, I'd realized it wasn't real, but from where I stood, it was my reality.

Living my life post-narcissist has been strange, unsettling and confusing. But the memories and triggers that bring me back to those years now fuel me to search deep within myself and check in about how I really feel about different situations and scenarios. Our time together wasn't the magic; the magic has been in the healing that I've done.

SEVEN

THE TAKE BACK

ON SEARCHING

AS I WAS WADING through transition, again, moving from uncomfortable but known and safe to uncomfortable and hopeful and optimistic, I spent hours sitting in my therapist's office crying. Over and over I would ask, "How do I get there faster?" I was stuck and I wanted to stop feeling terrible. I wanted answers, and I wanted to skip to the front of the line. I just wanted to be past this hard part.

"Have you ever meditated?" he asked. Uh, what? I wasn't going to meditate. I wanted a real answer. But it was a great question.

Historically, I'd been terrible at meditating; I either got antsy or fell asleep. What my therapist was telling me was to sit still and be quiet, to get rid of the chatter and noise so I could hear my own voice and intuition. He was telling me how to create space to be able to hear (and listen) to my own voice. It wasn't quite the magic bullet I was hoping for, but it was the best I had at that moment.

I realized at some point that the way Karl and I had quickly and decisively planned our wedding was either foreshadowing for the early days of parenthood or just really amazing practice. I had been so assertive and confident. I set the stage for the boundaries that I have now. I did those things subconsciously at first and then started to see the situations and interactions that had troubled me so much more clearly.

* * *

"What do you guys say about us when we leave?"

Do you have those friends or family or colleagues, or even acquaintances from school pick up, who you always feel judged by?

They have a way of prying that feels intrusive and puts you on high alert, on defense. Their judgy eyes seem to carry the weight of the world. Their critique feels like the universe is channeling disapproval through this person's voice to prove all the things you're doing wrong. Everyone knows what you're most afraid of, and they're proving why you're right…or why you're wrong, but correct about how wrong you are. When you ask, the world answers…usually in the form of some snarky "friend" eager to point out all the things that make you insecure or unsteady.

It feels like big inquisitive eyes staring at me, trying to peer into my brain and read my deepest thoughts, assuming they were about her, about the way other people did things. When we judge the world, I think we assume the world is also judging us. You might call this Step One of the "take back."

Karl and I had had dinner with some friends the night before. As I listened to the words echo from my speakerphone while I drove around town running errands, I was genuinely puzzled.

"Why would my husband and I talk about you guys after we leave dinner?" I replied. I imagine that as I said this my head was tilted and my eyes squinted a bit, as I do when I'm confused or trying to recall obscure details.

Whether it was dinner with friends, a PTA meeting, a work event or family gathering, this scenario feels all too familiar. The question was posed to me, but it could have just as easily been gossip about someone else. (Can you believe she did that? Can you believe they went there? Did you hear about the fight those two had?) It's a trap. It's dragging you into a world that isn't yours. It's giving you ownership and opinions and a stake in something that has nothing to do with you. But what it's really doing is opening the door for others to do the same. I realized that the follow-up question my friend was likely looking for was, "Well, what do you guys say about us?" An invitation to be told all of the things my husband and I were doing wrong in our marriage, as parents, at work, at the movies, at the restaurant, on vacation… anywhere really. It would have been an invitation for the judgments of anyone and everyone. But I didn't want it. I didn't need to give my opinion about someone else's relationship, and I wasn't looking for feedback on mine. Not everything needs outside interpretation. Or as I often tell my kids, "Don't be a jerk."

I've adopted this attitude in recent years, and it is literally life-changing! My ego wants to prove that I am always right. When I can tell that voice to shut it, I can let go of the need to be right, to be vindicated and validated. *I'm not going to be a jerk.*

The voice of my ego isn't me; it's all of my insecurities and my need for people to like and agree with me. It opens up the possibility that what other people like in me is not the same as what I like in me. That's the opposite of peace. That's a whole bunch of shit swirling around that can never settle and clear.

My ego wants to end every confrontation and argument with "and another thing" as I throw out more facts and knowledge and quotes and statistics, desperately needing an apology and acknowledgment of my right-ness and validation that I know everything.

My inner peace says "okay" and moves on. Do you want to go round after round about politics, judgments on the world, the sky is purple, the earth is flat, you were right, I was wrong? No. If we're having a productive conversation, that's one thing. If we're both committed to our beliefs and unwavering in our stance, then my ego is keeping me stuck in an unsolvable puzzle. A maze of frustration with no exit and no winning path. On the other hand, my inner peace says, *Okay*, with a smile that reflects how I feel about me and has nothing to do with you, *your willingness to join me doesn't impact where I'm going.*

When we're looking for validation, we jump into the conversations about other people. It confirms for us that at least we're not that bad. Once we jump in, it becomes circular and self-fulling. It's hard to get out. The world (the people in it, the loudest voices, expectations that are real or imagined, our inner assholes, social media, "influencers"), will ask for validation, and in return will judge your every move. This is a game I no longer play. I did for a long time, and it was terrible. So now I don't!

In my case, I sought out validation. I sought out acceptance. I crowdsourced my path. I assumed that the answers were outside of me, so that is where I searched—and I believed every single answer I found. I believed that what others had to say about my life and what I should or shouldn't be doing, feeling, enjoying or appreciating was, in fact, meant for me. And it wasn't.

I trusted the world because I didn't trust myself, and yet in hindsight I can see small glimpses of when I started trusting myself. It was out of character for me not to follow her strange question with a million others. To not ask her a question to glean some insight about how I should view her made-up situation. In this case, I didn't. My quiet, trusting voice was low key and intervened to stop the conversation. My subconscious was flexing a muscle I'd long abandoned.

You have to make your world yours—and like most other things, there's a fine line between owning your shit and being a jerk. Making your world yours means putting yourself at the center of your stuff—work, life, family, friends, goals, inspiration, expectations. Making it yours does not mean that you should be at the center of everything. You shouldn't be, and you aren't.

Today, I own what's mine and I leave the rest—but first, I got really, really clear about what was and wasn't mine. The weight of the world is an unnecessary burden, and no one needs it. I am not saying to approach life with a lack of compassion or understanding. I'm only saying that not everything is yours.

Some people are just jerks. They're cranky assholes wandering around the world trying to make everyone cranky with them—as if being around other people might somehow make them less of an asshole.

When we internalize everything and make it all about us (when it's not), it can be completely overwhelming. We become paralyzed by the weight of the world.

I can see a person in a grocery store being rude to someone working there, and I can either take that personally and assume their bad behavior is mine to feel and fix, or I can realize that it has nothing to do with me and instead say something kind to the worker. I can channel my feelings out of myself and to a place where they can actually help. I can simply say, "Thanks for your hard work, I appreciate it!" That's it.

The moments I wasn't able to do that, the ones where I internalized things, are the moments I have felt the least like myself.

I remember being in a dressing room with my good old friend Sarah, trying on clothes for a work conference we were attending. She slid a crewneck, cap-sleeve dress through the door.

"This would be great on you," she exclaimed.

My eyes must have seen this bullshit before my head did because every time I recount these scenarios there are moments when I just blink, as if my eyes are slowing down time so I can figure out what the fuck is happening.

I was in my late 20s at the time; I'm 40 years old now. If there is one thing I have known for damn sure my entire life, it is that I do not wear crewnecks or cap sleeves. It's something about the broad shoulders and big boobs I've had for as long as I can remember. In that particular style of garment, I look like a linebacker, and that is almost never the look I'm going for!

Reluctantly, I slid the dress on. It fit in the sense that I could zip it and still sit down, bend over and walk around. But it didn't fit.

I stepped out and said, "Eh, I don't love it." It looked hideous. That wasn't really an opinion; it was truly terrible.

"You're just scared because it's different, and you don't want to try something new," she said. "You can't wear jeans and a white T-shirt this time!" Fear as a motivation tactic is a real mindfuck.

I wasn't scared—I didn't like the dress! Often we hear about comfort zones, fear, resistance and the dangers of remaining "too comfortable." But sometimes people aren't pushing you out of your comfort zone because they want what's best for you. Sometimes people just get off on making you uncomfortable.

I see this a lot in the personal development space, and it even has a name: toxic positivity. Toxic positivity says "it's okay" when everything in your body is screaming that actually it's not. There's a whole world of self-help gurus all saying the same things:

Follow me for the path to enlightenment...

If I can do it, you can do it...

Here's what I did—it will work for you, too...

It gives the people hearing it a false sense of control. It's gurus trying—perhaps authentically, but often in a way that feels manipulative—to "empower" their followers. These people tell their acolytes that they can control their own future, that they can change their life, that there are finite rules and if they just follow them, they'll be able to...fill in the blank (with whatever the coach wants). What the people usually get in those scenarios is a guidebook they have to follow: step-by-step instructions, typically the ones that said guru prescribes and adheres to.

Don't get me wrong. I'm all for accountability, and there are definitely aspects of life you have control over. But this kind of "leadership" can be riddled with judgment and completely inflexible. Want more out of life? Work harder, wake up earlier, stop making excuses, *hustle, hustle, hustle*. If you end up doing all those things and still don't find the ultimate success you were promised, the next question the guru will ask is: were you really all in?

That advice is half a picture. It allows for no

nuance, no individuality and no personal circumstances. It presumes that everyone has everything they need to be successful and wants the same version of success, one that is equally attainable for everyone—oh, and that no one will ever change their mind or want to try something new.

It assumes you will find a role model in the form of a self-help or personal development guru and want to emulate them. But what if you don't? What if every alarm and buzzer and warning sign goes off in your body when you think about this? The "guru" might tell you you're scared, that you're letting fear hold you back. I've heard this. It's meant to shame you. And also, it's bullshit.

I felt certain that there was some specific thing I was supposed to do with my life and a very specific way that I was supposed to do it. I was constantly checking my surroundings for confirmation that I wasn't complying. Eventually I came to realize that my dependence on the world to validate me was in fact taking me even farther away from my true self. It felt safe to know that "the world" would approve, but I want to feel inner peace, calm and content. That's what puts a deep smile on my face. I wasn't going to find it doing what I assumed others would want me to do.

I am worthy, capable and valid, no matter what

anyone else says. My path to fulfillment is built entirely on how much I'm willing to trust myself. It's built on how much weight I'm willing to give my own voice and intuition, and that means keeping anything that threatens those things at arm's length. I spent years of my life believing so many lies about what it meant to be a wife, a mother, a friend and a business owner. They were lies that permeated my mindset because I hadn't yet learned to listen to my own voice.

By believing in myself and my abilities, I'm not seeking outside validation or input on my decisions. It doesn't mean that I assume I know everything, and I don't ever discount research or expert opinions. But I don't need a million facts and data points to justify what I'm doing. I trust my instincts and believe in my ability to course-correct as needed. I don't waste valuable time staying on a path (or standing at a fork in the road) while other possibilities and opportunities pass me by.

Like anything else, trusting your instincts is a learned behavior. I trust my instincts, and the more I trust them, the more I can depend on them. I firmly believe that when I'm making a decision for myself or my family, if it feels right, then it probably is. This goes for decisions big and small. When my husband and I were planning our wedding, we visited two venues, and we met one photographer, one florist and one DJ.

When we bought our first house, we looked at two houses. When we bought our current house, it was the only one we saw.

I don't expect that life is going to be easy, or that making decisions is going to be easy. I do expect that I'm going to listen to myself and trust myself. I expect that I'm never going to let someone else's voice become louder than my own.

I expect that I'm never going to hesitate to put an ugly dress that doesn't fit back on the rack.

EIGHT
I JOINED A CULT...AND IT CHANGED MY LIFE
ON WORK, AGAIN

MY FATHER-IN-LAW HAS BEEN KNOWN to say, "Never let the truth get in the way of a good story," so the title of this chapter is a bit of a "Schwarzbellishment" (a term coined by my sister-in-law).

I didn't join a cult, but I did join a direct sales company in 2015.

My network marketing "success story" isn't about diamonds and trips and six-figure paychecks. I didn't build a huge team, gain fame and glory within the company or "retire" my husband. When I joined the company, those weren't the things I was looking for—at least not entirely. What I was drawn to, and desperately in need of without entirely realizing it, was a purpose, a community and a next step. I know there are distinctions between them, but for the purposes of this section, I use the terms *direct sales*, *MLM* (multi-level marketing) and *network marketing* interchangeably.

I knew I needed to be around people, and I definitely knew that I was not looking to go back to a corporate job. The only things I could picture were images that had already been painted: other women and other stories.

While I am not a huge fan of this saying, I've often referred to direct sales as a "gateway drug" into entrepreneurship, which was a little taste of something I knew I needed more of! In job interviews and annual reviews in the corporate world, the question was always inevitable:

"Where do you see yourself in five years?"

They weren't asking about my hopes and dreams, where I wanted to travel, what I wanted to learn and experience and become outside of the office. They didn't care about what books I wanted to read or how I'd make myself a better person. They weren't necessarily interested in the person I was becoming. The question in that context was simply, "Will you still work hard and do this job in five years?"

That was okay; it was simply how things worked in corporate America. Still, I was starting to feel aware enough to have a list of things I wanted and didn't want from whatever move I'd make next. I needed people and community. I needed those people to not be cranky. I needed a bit of accountability but not managing. I wanted something fun and exciting and new. I wanted somewhere I could feel smart and funny and capable. I knew that it was time to shake things up a bit.

When I was a doula, my work life was centered on the birth of babies. Because babies aren't born on a nine-to-five, Monday through Friday schedule, neither was I—which made trying to maintain the schedules of three kids, a husband and a dog quite difficult. After I left the world of doula work, I tried my hand at being a real estate agent. Even more than the around-the-clock schedule, I needed a shift that was decidedly different and put me at the center of whatever step I was going to take next.

I remember a friend asking, "How do you go from being a doula to being a real estate agent?"

It happened pretty quickly, actually; a friend of a friend had been looking to hire an agent in my area, and our mutual connection had a hunch I'd be good at the job. The work itself was surprisingly similar to what I'd done as a doula. It was slightly less intimate and rarely involved middle-of-the-night phone calls, but in both roles, I helped people navigate incredibly scary and overwhelming situations, often for the first time. The end results were life-changing, but the process itself could be super bumpy.

In both my work as a doula and a real estate agent, I brought my knowledge, resources and experience to my clients but had no vested interest in the decisions they made. It wasn't about me. Instead, I had the opportunity to be potentially the only person who'd just be there for them in the process.

* * *

I was good at being a real estate agent and I liked doing it, but it didn't stick. It wasn't my forever path, and after a few years, I felt the familiar urge to look for something new. In the middle of 2015, an acquaintance introduced me to a direct sales company, and I was quickly intrigued by both the work and the narrative surrounding it.

When I started selling eye cream, my potential and options seemed to be about who I was and what I wanted—to do, to learn, to experience, to accomplish. While I don't necessarily have an issue with every single direct sales company, there are more than a few that practice less-than-ethical tactics and ones that definitely have a cult-like feel, and fair or not, that can create cultures that feel unsavory. Many direct sales companies encourage representatives to spend money they don't have on supplies and stock, and many of them also make it seem like effort and attitude are all you need to succeed. If you're not succeeding, it then follows that it must be your fault.

I've seen amazing women (and men) accomplish incredible things in direct sales, and I buy from and support many friends who do it. It can be a respectable way to create a life for some people within some companies. Still, *LuLaRich* and various other documentaries about MLMs have shown just how closely MLMs can mirror cults. Some are super shady, some are downright criminal and some are just weird (leggings with fucking cheeseburgers on them, anyone?).

For many people—especially women and people who feel lonely, left out and lacking something in their lives—I believe they offer something that isn't easily found anywhere else—but not without some serious conditionality.

As with anything else, there are shitty companies in stand-up industries and there are good, solid companies within shady industries; the same thing goes for people, policies and cultures. In some cases, the good far outweighs the bad, and in others, well, the owner of your company blacklists you when you don't get bariatric surgery in Tijuana, as anyone who watched the Amazon documentary *LuLaRich* knows.

From my perspective, the company (and specifically, the team within that company) I was part of was among the more reputable, with seemingly solid leadership and legit products. Most things tend to look better from afar, and that's where I was. And I also like to change my mind and try new things, and that doesn't necessarily fit into the model of direct sales. It isn't a career path you can meander through, weaving in and out and possibly finding yourself on a different path toward a different destination. It's a train on a track. You're the driver, but if you see a destination in the distance that your tracks don't lead to, you might have to jump off or potentially abandon that other vision.

I like to wander, and I don't like to be herded back to the pack, but it can feel shitty to have to leave everyone and everything behind in order to get to a destination that's better suited to you. It can make the whole thing feel like it wasn't real in the first place—like who you were wasn't actually you. And if you build your life, world and confidence based on who you are in the context of that company and then that context changes, what does that leave you with?

The personal development component of direct sales was not something I was expecting. I joined for the products, community and ability to make money. I'd be remiss if I didn't also say that I was adamantly opposed to going back to a corporate job. I couldn't fathom going to an office every day—at least not someone else's office—so I wanted and needed this to work. And then I felt a shift. I started reading books about personal growth and development and thinking about things in a different way. I stopped seeing myself as someone who needed to be fixed and started seeing myself as someone to explore and uncover, someone filled with potential. I just had to figure out how to act on it.

At first, all of the conversations I had with myself and other people came back to the product: in direct sales, personal development is directly tied to success in the business. If I was talking to somebody who didn't want to be a consultant on my team, or someone who wasn't going to buy products, in that model, they didn't fit into my world.

Or they did...but they weren't supposed to. In theory and in the words I heard, I was supposed to talk to everyone because "you never know" who might want to buy facial cleanser and eventually join my team so they could sell facial cleanser, too. I was supposed to be interested in them and what they needed and wanted and then, in a subtle and genuine kind of way, I was supposed to talk about the products or business. That seemed neither subtle nor genuine. It created a sense of failure, in large part because I wasn't trying hard enough, but also the not trying hard enough came from the fact that I was actually listening when I started these conversations—this wasn't what they needed or wanted. Bringing up this "amazing opportunity" was about what I wanted. So I missed goals, a lot. This felt terrible, but in hindsight it was also a huge relief.

What if I wanted to talk about hopes and wants and fears and needs with all the same people but not sell eye cream and serums? What if I wanted to train and inspire people, but I didn't care if they joined the company or bought the products? What if I just thought they were awesome and should have the same fire breathed into them that the "new recruits" got? What about the people who were looking for something but found that direct sales wasn't it? What happened to them? How could I help them? What about the people who needed and deserved support and community but didn't want to join a business? They deserved all of the good stuff, too! Direct sales is obviously a sales job—what was I supposed to do if I met someone with whom I felt a connection but did not feel a potential sale? I liked the products I was selling, but what I loved was making connections. Could I have one without the other?

These questions swirled around in my head, and then finally, I got stuck on one that I ultimately ended up asking myself, over and over:

What if I change my mind?

I held on to the good I was getting out of this business and kept pushing forward...for five and a half years.

I remember once having a conversation with a friend of mine. I'd known her for years, and she was one of the smartest women I knew. So confident, so sure of herself—generally just really awesome. Also, she was exactly the kind of woman I should be talking to about this amazing opportunity I had. She was in between jobs and had *zero* interest in an MLM. So much of it made sense, the concept of what I thought she deserved, but it also needed to exist in a different package to actually be what she needed and wanted.

"You're so smart and good at what you do, it seems infuriating that you have to wait for someone else to want to hire you. You should get to decide where you want to work and just make it happen!" I was saying this because, as it turns out, that's exactly how an MLM works. This was convenient for the point I was trying to make, but I was also making a big assumption that this was the place where she'd want to work. I was drawing a straight line where a direct path didn't necessarily exist. It's like being hungry and someone offers you food you hate. Sure, the food is a good solution to the general problem you have, but it doesn't solve your actual dilemma.

I could see the problem, and I could offer as a possible solution. But I could also see so much more.

The me who was being a genuine friend and actually engaged in a conversation had all kinds of solutions and options and ideas to offer up. But the me who was looking for my next promotion and trying to earn some prize or trip or sparklier lanyard at a convention only had a single thing to offer, and I knew all the ways to handle any objection thrown my way. But I didn't want to.

The internal and outward dialogues sometimes differed, at odds and fighting for control.

I knew what I got out of this business, and I knew what others could get from it, too, but I also knew that it wasn't what everyone was looking for. The narrowness of what it can be, or rather how it could be done, was a deal breaker—at first for others and ultimately for me.

There were guidelines around conversations, which I'd been exposed to a bit in real estate, too. Mostly, these dialogue scripts intended to move a conversation along, relaying all the good information quickly to help people arrive at an answer—or rather, helping them arrive at the answer I hoped for.

Meet new people, start conversations every day... these were my marching orders. I understand the words. But they don't feel authentic, and they don't feel like me. I don't meet new people every day. I'm not opposed to talking to strangers (sometimes) in the line at the coffee shop or while waiting for a salad, but the notion that I'd always do this with anyone and everyone, no matter what kind of magic I had to offer them, is silly. I'm selectively chatty or antisocial by choice.

I started asking myself the question, "If I had nothing to gain from this conversation—they have no interest in business, no interest in products, have a competing or similar business and would never support or add to my business—would I still engage in this conversation? Am I genuinely, eagerly excited to talk to this person, or am I excited to see if I can help them in a way that actually helps me?"

The thing I know about myself is that I do not move well through misalignment. When my words and my feelings aren't in alignment, I tend to stop talking.

"You'd be so great at this" but you might also hate it.

"The products sell themselves!" as long as you talk about them *a lot*.

"You can make some great extra money" but you might think about this all day every day.

"It's such an amazing opportunity, and can become whatever you make it," sort of.

What's missing from these conversations is the nuance. My Enneagram 7 brain works in big pictures and nuance. I see big, broad ideas—and then I see a thousand little ways to get there.

I stuck around for longer than I wanted to because although I knew direct sales wasn't going to be it for me, I didn't know where else to find that kind of connection and shared interest in growth anywhere else. Sellers would go to a convention every year; where else would you have an opportunity to share a hotel room with three of your best friends and be allowed to really peer into yourself? Where else could I be in community with people who were different from me but whose goals were the same as mine?

I like to change my mind. I'm comfortable outgrowing situations and stepping into new spaces. But I like to keep my people. We don't have to stay on the same path or go at the same speed, but as a 40-year-old woman who is afraid of the dark, literally and metaphorically, I like some familiar faces around.

For me, direct sales was a gift. It opened my eyes to so much I hadn't previously seen before. But—and read this next piece twice:

It wasn't something I was doing to support my family financially.

The income was secondary to all the rest. I had the freedom to explore the sales path and take advantage of opportunities and experiences, which is not everyone's reality. And that's where these kinds of businesses can be super detrimental. The ideas they promote that "anyone can do this" are a bit naive and actually require more nuance. Can anyone do it and be "successful" (meaning climb to the top of the ladder)? Maybe. But does everyone have the same time, resources and network to create meaningful income? Not necessarily.

And also, some people are looking for friendship and the community, and it isn't until you're in it for a certain amount of time that you realize your "success" is required to really be part of those things, at least to some extent. When you join for community but then find there's a path you have to follow in order to gain access to that community, it can be a shock to the system. The instinct is to fight and bend and twist to try to make yourself fit, even though it may not be your path.

In my case, I was able to participate in the "pay to play" aspect of the business. I didn't need a thriving business to be able to attend events and conventions or to dive into personal development courses and books. Of course, what I was looking for (and found) through the journey was also what made it possible and necessary for me to leave.

I often start sentences with "My friend in Boise," "A woman I know in Montana" or "My friend, the chemist slash recovery coach in Oregon."

Aside from the five years I lived in Boston and the six months I lived in New York City, I have spent my entire life in Westchester County, New York, and most people I know either live or have lived in the state of New York. I might never have had an occasion to make friends with people in Boise, Montana, Oregon, but I did—and that's just a geographical representation of the randomness that has become part of my world over the past six years.

In theory, I had no reason to be regularly logging onto Zoom calls before March 2020, and yet by that time, Zoom was already a huge part of my life and my connection to friends, people who felt so close while being physically far away. I won't say that past experience made it easier to navigate the pandemic or those early days of just being home in March and April 2020, but it definitely gave me a strong belief in what was possible, a confidence in knowing how emotionally close people actually could be at a distance. I'd already forged relationships in virtual space through direct sales and the people and events that have, over the last few decades, popped up around it.

When I left the direct sales company I was involved with, I worried that I would also be walking away from the connections I'd made and the work I was doing not to sell products but to get to know myself. I won't lie: in many cases, when you leave direct sales, you're gone—the people who are still in it don't want anything to do with you. I feel lucky that I was able to make some genuine connections and friendships that are still a part of my life. One of them was the first person I told I'd quit drinking. Of course, on the plane to go meet some of them in person for the first time, I wondered to myself if maybe I was a little nuts. We knew some really deep, intense stuff about each other, but what if the dynamic was totally different in person?

In the summer of 2018, I took a $47, 14-day challenge with a woman who was involved in direct sales—but she was also definitely doing her own thing and pursuing her own business goals, which I found very appealing. Later that year, she offered a more in-depth course and it felt, for the first time, like I was doing what I was truly supposed to be doing. A year later in summer 2019, a smaller group of us committed to a year-long program, which is how I found myself en route to Boise for the first time.

I'd traveled alone before, but it had usually been to meet a best friend at the destination. It had never been to meet a bunch of "strangers." They didn't feel like strangers, of course, but we had never shared physical space. Karl, I think, was perplexed.

"You're going to share a hotel room with people

you've never met?" was a common refrain in the weeks leading up to my departure. But suddenly, there I was boarding my second flight of the day, all alone and on my way to what would become four of the most impactful days of my life with a bunch of women I only knew through the internet.

I made the trip again in 2021, after two more years of communicating exclusively through the computer, and it was like no time had passed. The relationships I have with these women are unique; I might not know the names of their kids, and they might not know the names of mine, but we know powerful, deep stuff about one another.

It was through the work I did with my coaching group that I came back to my goal of wanting to write words that other people would read. I started a Facebook group; it was the next step to saying, "I have things to say, and I think people might be interested in hearing them." It felt like a safe space. The people there were the people I knew were interested in me and what I was thinking about, and posting there helped me push past some of the self-consciousness that always exists when you're putting yourself out there for the first time. I've learned with other people who, like me, try on a bunch of stuff that almost fits.

And to think it all started with a jar of eye cream.

NINE
INSTAGRAM VERSUS REALITY
ON SOCIAL MEDIA

"THAT! THAT'S WHAT I WANT," I say in a hushed whisper as I scroll through her Instagram feed. I can envision myself in that outfit with that cheeky smile as I laugh, carefree and oozing happiness and confidence. But it's a picture. A single, captured moment in time. A posed moment in time.

I never stop to think what might be hiding behind those bright eyes. I'm drawn to the image while everything behind it feels irrelevant, and that snarky voice inside my head is saying if she got it, you can get it...but you'd probably already have it if you were capable. I sigh and keep scrolling.

The "her" I'm referring to could be any one of the beautiful, put together, creative moms I see on Instagram's Explore page on any given day. It doesn't really matter who she is because there are tons of her.

Right now, in this strange technologically fueled world we live in, influencers and curators of life (sometimes we don't even know what to call them) are everywhere. They can fit into many different boxes: mom down the street, famous self-help "guru," actor, reality TV celebrity, blogger, writer, podcaster or just a straight-up influencer—famous for the sake of being famous and getting people to buy stuff. Their words carry extra weight, their endorsements bring validation and any similarities you can draw to them bestow a sense of worth and acceptance.

A friend of mine wrote a book called *Highlight Real*, and in it, she gets, well, very real. She also talks about the highlight reel she'd previously been creating in her social media feed. As her world was falling apart, spectators could and likely did mutter enviously beneath their breath as they scrolled through her carefully curated images and admired the fun-loving, happy-go-lucky mom of five. But to what end? They wanted the picture, not the journey or the life. I wanted that picture. I desperately wanted what she had, or what I thought she had. Most of the women we idolize through the internet don't pull back the curtains to show us the real story. I feel incredibly lucky that Emily didn't stop with the picture-perfect images and gave the full story. She opened the door for me to feel more and be more and see more.

In old movies and TV shows, it's not uncommon to see characters reading the newspaper in the morning to find out what happened the previous 24 hours. That image now seems a million miles away from the constant real-time onslaught of information and updates we receive through the internet and social media. Combined with the rapid-fire information, images, and thoughts coming at us from influencer and self-help culture, we're facing an onslaught of "shoulds." The rise of influencers and self-help personalities are converging with the exponential speeds of information delivery through social media in a way that is blurring the lines between shame and inspiration. We are entering strange new territory, and it can feel overwhelming.

Social media can create and enable connection, information sharing and camaraderie in a way I'm not sure anyone would ever have imagined—a way that isn't necessarily replicable in the real world. The relationships I've been able to foster online and the closeness and connection made possible despite physical distance have been life-changing and amazing. Even so, social media is kind of trash.

People can be terrible, information can be wrong and everything can be fake. It's like walking into a funhouse with all the wonky mirrors but not actually knowing that's what it is. Social media is a place to practice self-trust and critical thinking; you can't wander naively through this strange land. It's also a place where I work on centering and understanding where I'm coming from. It means looking at images and reading captions and knowing when it's for me and when it's not, when I should let the words in and when I should keep scrolling.

Social media is a part of life for all of my kids. We have rules and expectations about how to behave with and around social media, but I think the real lessons for how to interact on the internet happen offline. The ways my kids interact with people and world around them, what is and is not acceptable in our house and our family, all feeds into how they exist in the online space. The line between online and offline is blurry, but our code of conduct can't be based on one standard in one world and a different one in the other. How you treat people, how you speak, who and what you believe, the things you accept and the things you stand up against should be (largely) universal across all realms. Much of what we see online doesn't impact us in real life, so when we fixate on and generate tons of internal energy about it, we create a disconnect between our emotions and what we really care about.

The same thing is true of TV or movies or books. As a teenager, it felt like I lived and died in the drama of *Beverly Hills, 90210* and *Melrose Place*; as an adult,

I stopped watching *Grey's Anatomy* and *This Is Us* because I couldn't handle the emotional rollercoaster— I still get teary-eyed thinking of Mark Sloan and Lexi and their tortured dramas. And those are TV shows, of course; they are not real!

The conversations I have with my kids and myself about social media start with the understanding that you can most definitely have real feelings and emotions about things that aren't real, but you need to be able to understand the difference. I can be sad about the unfulfilled dreams that were cut short for my favorite doctors on a TV show and also snap myself back to reality because my line between real and not real is very clear. With social media, it's a very different story. Everything feels real, looks real and is validated by things that actually are real.

I appreciate the internet and social media for what they are. I take the good stuff, leave the bad stuff and try to make sure that my instincts stay sharp enough to see the difference. And like most other things in life, I narrate the process to take my kids along for the ride.

When we play follow the leader with an overly curated "influencer," the assumptions we make and the expectations we create for ourselves and others result in a life and world where we're constantly trying to beat a score that doesn't even exist. It keeps us playing a game alone and wondering why we keep coming in last.

It's not like things are any better on the other side of the fence. How many Insta-moms have shared stories about depression, parenting struggles and anxieties? How many divorce announcements have I seen, carefully written so as not to reveal anything more than "we'll always be best friends and co-parents" beneath a dreamy picture supposed to communicate "starting over"? I'm not talking about schadenfreude—and if you've never heard the word schadenfreude, don't feel bad; I hadn't either until I read Brené Brown's latest book *Atlas of the Heart*, which has a fascinating section about this word. I take no pleasure in seeing real-life trials and tribulations come to people I follow for outfit inspiration. I just mean that every time I feel bad about myself, someone, somewhere, is feeling bad about herself, too.

The hardest years of my life were the ones where I felt like I needed (and thus became desperate for) validation for every aspect of my life. In some instances, I was actually saying the words, "What do you think about…?" and then feeling stuck within the bubble of those answers. In others, I would look at the world around me, make assumptions and judgments and create my own, equally stifling bubbles, planting myself suffocatingly inside.

When my oldest child Mia was four months old, I used to go to a new mom support group. It was hosted in a local doula's basement and was everything a new mom needed: validation, support, companionship and judgment-free ears to listen. Mia was a happy and outgoing baby, and I remember the woman saying to me once, "As this baby grows, you should ask her, 'But how do you feel about x, y, z?' often." She was picking up on my easygoing nature, my tendency to sometimes lose myself or become too adaptable.

Today, I try to stand firmly and confidently in most aspects of my life. I don't question my decisions, I don't question my actions and I don't question my parenting. I'm definitely not saying that I feel rock-solid belief in everything I do, but there are certain aspects of life on which I do not seek outside opinions (though yes, I do still send pics of outfit choices to my besties). The more I focus on living within that space—the space where I'm not anxiously checking to see how many people "like" my content—the more I feel confidently like myself.

TEN
THERE'S NO BOAT
ON WHAT'S NEXT

IN THE UNIVERSE of *The Golden Girls*, Rose was supposed to be 55 when the show started in 1985. It was on the air until 1992, so she'd have been 62 when it ended—in her "golden years." They were grandmas who stuffed Kleenex in their sleeves and reprimanded youngsters for being unruly. Blanche and Dorothy were both 53.

There's a lot to love about these women, but the vision they create for a 20-something woman watching the show can be confusing. They're awesome, badass ladies, totally ahead of their time in so many ways, and yet they make 53 seem a million miles away. But 53 is only far away until it's not. Until you're approaching 40 and realize you have just over a decade left of keeping your hair long, dark and flowy. Until you realize your days of yoga pants are coming to an end, and it's time to start shopping for a bunch of holiday-themed sweatshirts and quilted housecoats.

Women in Hollywood go from bombshell to grandma with one birthday as the men become more dashing and debonair with silver streaks and rugged laugh lines. Women hear biological clocks ticking while wrestling with sagging boobs, wrinkles and gray hair. While it's definitely starting to shift, youth is still the ideal. And for a long time, I was the youngest, by a lot, everywhere I went.

It felt special. I worked in a restaurant when I was 14, and I graduated from high school in three years, making me a 17-year-old college freshman. I did my first college internship at 18 and my second at 19, working that job until I was 21. I was smart and did well and was always between five and 25 years younger than my coworkers. My age was always a point of note, in large part because we had to be strategic about which happy hour we could go to when I was underage.

There's a freedom and desirability about youth and all that it is perceived to entail. It's not the reality of it, but it's the idea, which makes it even worse. Somehow 26 is elusive, exotic and sexy. It's also young—really young! And then it's over, and you look around the room and realize you're no longer the youngest person there. The fact that you're smart and have things to say and opinions worth hearing? No longer noteworthy! What else are you bringing to the table?

The day after I turned 40, 39 suddenly seemed so young! How could it be possible that just the day before, I was young and spry with my whole life ahead of me, and now I was 40? I'm being dramatic. Obviously there is plenty of life still ahead of 40, but I did feel a sense of doom and dread. I didn't even necessarily believe there was any truth in what I was feeling; I just thought I was supposed to believe this.

When I was 30, friends of ours were moving out of state and had planned a going-away party...at a karaoke bar. I don't like karaoke and never have. I sing in the car, at concerts and when I'm home alone. I sing when there is no microphone and very few other ears to hear me.

Most of the women there were more than a decade older than me. I remember watching as they sang their little hearts out to Bon Jovi, Joan Jett and Guns N' Roses. I didn't sing, and I remember wondering if the way they sang and danced and smiled was something earned for passing your 40th birthday. I wondered if 10 years in the future I would be able to stand up in front of friends and family and belt out the hits of my youth without caring how I sounded or looked.

I've since passed that milestone. It didn't come with the desire to do karaoke, but it definitely came with the freedom to not give a fuck about a lot of things.

It's funny how strange moments can stick in your mind. That night in a karaoke bar has stuck with me for more than a decade. I had watched these women—my friends—embody something that felt so foreign to me at the time. It gave me a twinge of excitement for what the next decade would bring, for who I'd become...and yet, I also spent the next nine and a half years feeling a bit of dread. What the fuck was that all about?

As I think about it, it was probably some combination of feeling like I'd soon become irrelevant and that I'd missed the opportunity to climb aboard a magic boat and sail away into the sunset. Perhaps it had shown up when I wasn't looking to take me to "my path," and I'd missed it. My way to the elusive success we're all supposed to want.

Up until very recently, lists were "20 under 20" and "30 under 30." Mika Brzezinski and her Know Your Value initiative partnered with *Forbes* last year to start their "50 over 50" to honor women who've accomplished great things over 50, either through a pivot or through perseverance. Imagine that. Imagine approaching your mid-40s, mid-50s, and mid-60s and being told by the world that you can still create and still pivot.

Part of why I felt the loss of wanting to be a writer so keenly in that bar in Boston was that I assumed, on some level, that I was already too late. That if I hadn't begun a writing career by then, I never would. But here I am, writing my first book at 40—hopefully, the first of many. I spent so long assuming I'd missed the boat, but what if there was no boat to begin with?

I attended a virtual retreat last year led by my friend, the brilliant Jen Pastiloff. One of our exercises was a vision casting to imagine the future 10 years out. It wasn't a new exercise for me. I'd taken a lot of writing workshops, and so I'd done it dozens of times before—but at that moment, and probably for the first time ever, it was different. There was something really exciting and freeing about putting those words on paper.

I realized that 10 years into the future, I'd be 49. My initial thought when I sat down to write that was yikes, I'll be a few months away from 50! That shifted from a feeling of dread to one of possibility and excitement.

I'd be an empty nester. My youngest would be a freshman in college. I love and adore my children, but that shift in the perception of my future reality felt overwhelmingly full of possibility. It was a new chapter that would unfold. All of the other times I'd done the exercise, I'd had little kids, so the future still revolved around being a mom of littles; I'd be in different stages of being a mom to young kids, but that was still the overarching theme. This time, it felt like it was about me!

So, here's my vision for the life of Lauren Schwarzfeld, in the year 2031:

I am 49 years old. My kids are all out of high school and stepping into the fullest versions of themselves, or at least taking bigger steps in that direction.

I live in California.

I am a writer, a speaker, a leader.

I am happy and content.

I write outside.

I am loved.

I am respected.

I am trusted.

I have meaningful relationships.

I connect daily with people who appreciate me.

I am generous.

I support the people and causes I believe in.

I travel often, for work and rest.

I feel light and alive.

I *allow*:

Love

Respect

Knowledge

Newness

Affection

Opportunities

Time alone

Beauty, in nature and in my home

Endless books

Endless time to read books

Time to write

Time to appreciate my body

Peace

Relationships that fuel me

Fresh air, time outside every day

Change, as necessary

Money to spend on things that are important to my soul

New experiences

Experiences to end when they're supposed to

Without realizing it, I was creating a new belief around age at a time when I desperately needed it. I'm not going to lie: I was freaking out about turning 40. It sounds and feels ridiculous, but it makes sense given the world we live in. The gift this exercise became was a reframing, one that created a new set of emotions and beliefs around what was still to come and what I could still accomplish and feel and experience.

The fear that has been instilled and then exacerbated by social media is that if we don't do everything right this minute, we will miss out. The lessons of life itself say exactly the opposite. It's in trying to do everything all at once that the missing out happens. How on earth can you experience the beauty and pain and laughter and heartbreak of something if you're not giving it your full attention?

The noise of the world is trying to rush us. It's trying to tell us that any opportunities we get are fleeting and once in a lifetime. *Do this, or you'll regret it forever.* It is trying to take over our internal voice, and age is such an easy way to trick us.

Think about how often pictures of female celebrities go viral simply because the celebrity in question looks conventionally hot and also has the nerve to be over 50. I'm not going to say women like Jennifer Lopez don't have amazing genes (and/or amazing plastic surgeons), but what if the reason she looks amazing at 50 is because 50-year-old women are more than capable of looking—and being—amazing? Thirty-nine might feel young to 40-year-old me, but I'm learning that 40 feels pretty young, too!

I know in a decade, I'll look back at this hand-wringing and laugh. I know that I'll feel differently, but I also know I'll have a whole decade's worth of experiences to look back on, and rather than mourn the time that has passed, I hope more than anything that I'm still excited for what's to come.

***

The new moms group I went to after Mia was born feels, in some ways, like it happened yesterday. Sitting in a cozy basement with other new moms and a dear friend hosting, we'd laugh and cry, drink coffee and eat freshly baked muffins, just passing the time on a Tuesday morning. I can't remember what led to the one particular morning we were vision casting, journaling about our future lives.

I do remember in great detail the words I wrote; I remember them because they feel ingrained in me. For years, I had done the exercise in different settings, and it always sounded the same. I'd write and write and write; then as I looked back at the words, I'd realize that I'd already written them. They were visions I'd already had but had only remembered when thinking about the future.

Sunday morning, present day, I sit down in my office to write and realize that I am living the words I wrote so many times. Years ago, I stopped trying to get those visions to become reality. It simply didn't feel like they would ever be mine. I look up from my laptop for a moment to take a sip of coffee and am struck with déjà vu—the music, the smells, the window, the white desk and comfy chairs. The sleeping kids (though in the present, it's because they're teens and pre-teens, and sleeping in isn't as much of a treat as it was when I first wrote about it). Here I am, 13, 15, 17 years out from all those "Fuck, I'm in the wrong spot" realizations, and a sense of peace is washing over me. I asked for this, and then I let it happen.

I am far, far away from the girl who made the very logical decisions in my late teens and early 20s. I'm past the "good on paper" decisions, the things I can prove and explain. I am now the woman who deeply trusts herself and believes that I can make stuff work. I can create magic if I let myself. I know when I'm on the right path, and I know when it's time to shift.

I created the life I needed. And suddenly, I belonged.

ACKNOWLEDGMENTS

Mia, Jacob & Abigail...three of my most favorite people. I am so grateful that I get to be on this journey with you. So much of the work I did in writing this book, and in the years of practice that led me to being able to write it, came from a desire to show you three how much you matter—to me and to yourselves.

Katy, Kate the Great, my sister. My first best friend. The most amazing aunt to my kids and my forever person. I had no idea how lucky I am to have you as my sister, but there is literally nothing we can't do together...even if we giggle too often and inappropriately.

Thank you to my mom, Cynthia. The best mom and grandma there is. Your ability, willingness and deep desire to take care of me and my kids has truly allowed us to be who we are. We love you, we're grateful for you and we're so happy we get to have you so close!

Meghan Milano, everyone deserves a friend and cheering section like you. Your friendship means more to me than I can say, but I love you and appreciate you for always having my back and always having the words I need to hear.

Emily Paulson, I think I've run out of ways to express my gratitude for everything you've done for me and the ways you've inspired me and helped me navigate the past five years. I will never be able to repay all you've given me but will forever be grateful that you found your way into my world.

Sara Manes and Bec Martin, you were the first two people to read this book and every previous iteration (to read most of what I write, actually). There's something so special about friends we make as adults, the friends that don't come about by way of convenience or geography. The ones that are just meant to be and somehow find each other.

Jen Pastiloff, your words inspire me and continue to light a fire within my soul. I am deeply grateful for your friendship and for the way you make this world a better place. Your words, "May I have the courage to be who I say I am" have carried me through the writing of this book and continue to carry me into whatever is next. Your workshops opened something within me that made this book both necessary and possible.

Anna David and the Legacy Launch Pad Team, the opportunity to bring dreams to life is an unparalleled feeling and you've all made this possible. Anna, you've created something amazing in this company and I'm so honored to be part of it.

Angela Serratore, there is something so special about incredibly smart friends who can also talk endlessly about trashy TV and I adore you for it! I can't thank you enough for helping me along this process.

ABOUT THE AUTHOR

Lauren Schwarzfeld is a coach and writer whose work has appeared online and in the bestselling anthology *The Addiction Diaries*. In her coaching practice, she helps her clients reclaim space in their own lives, step out of their perceived expectations and learn to trust themselves. Schwarzfeld lives in Mount Kisco, New York with her husband Karl, their three children Mia, Jacob and Abigail and their two dogs, Felix and Edna. *Unboxed* is her first book.

Made in United States
North Haven, CT
11 March 2022

17012510R00098